**30 days.
30 exercises.
30 results that will transform
your marriage.**

*Includes simple techniques for . . .*

- Letting go of unrealistic expectations
- Detecting hidden messages in marital
  communication
- Welcoming your spouse back into your life
- Appreciating each other's unique qualities
  And more

# 30 DAYS TO A HAPPIER
MARRIAGE

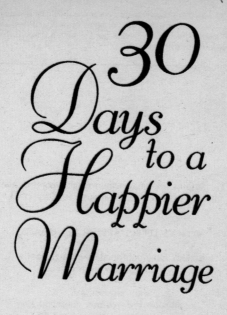

# 30 Days to a Happier Marriage

**Jay Gale, Ph.D., &
Sheila Taurone, M.A.**

BERKLEY BOOKS, NEW YORK

The authors gratefully acknowledge Dennis Tordini for the original art that appears in Chapter 13.

30 DAYS TO A HAPPIER MARRIAGE

A Berkley Book/published by arrangement with Longmeadow Press

PRINTING HISTORY
Longmeadow Press edition published 1992
Berkley edition / November 1995

BERKLEY®
Berkley Books are published by The Berkley Publishing Group,
200 Madison Avenue, New York, New York 10016.
BERKLEY and the "B" design
are trademarks belonging to Berkley Publishing Corporation.

PRINTED IN THE UNITED STATES OF AMERICA

10 9 8 7 6 5 4 3 2 1

*For Mom & Dad,*
*and for Herb & Annette—*
*with thanks for sharing the love*
*and joy that have given Fran and me*
*the tools and the gifts*
*to make our marriage what it is*

—J.G.


*For Dominic,*
*Stephanie,*
*and Cassandra—*
*for teaching*
*me lessons in*
*loving*

—S.T.

# CONTENTS

# ACKNOWLEDGMENTS

The knowledge and wisdom accumulated in this book is the legacy of more than one thousand patients who have inspired us with their willingness to share the pain and the joy in their lives. We thank them for what we, too, have learned in the process.

We are also grateful to our family of friends at La Paz Psychological Group and La Paz Family Recovery Services for their support and feedback; especially Nancy Recht, Karen Mazzarese, Manny Tau, Jerry Smith, Marge Veal, and extended family members Peter Sukin and Sharon Roy.

A few special people also stand out for time and contributions during the process of putting this book together: Donna Hobbs, Dorette Morris, Ann Aarhaus, R. C. Shades, and Leslie McMaster, as well as Ann Marie O'Farrell, whose faith in the concept of this book made it into a reality.

Of course, both of us are forever thankful to our spouses, Fran and Dominic, for their unwavering faith, constant encouragement, and tremendous assistance in editing and thinking through our material.

And a special thank you from Sheila to the Friday night group and Andrew Casey for their years of loving support and direction; to Karen Bohan, Francie Latimore, Val Jon Farris, and Cynthia Stevens for their challenge to continue the inner child work; and to Ginny Gordon and Marcia Margolis for their love and their wonderful minds.

# INTRODUCTION

## The Thirty-Day Program

Thirty days to a happier marriage? For anyone who has ever been married, this has to seem like a lie. It doesn't seem possible.

What about all the warnings about the hard work involved in establishing a marriage? Well, that part is true. After all, our title doesn't say anything about not having to work at your marriage, and it doesn't say that after the thirty days are over you can sit back and just relax.

Based upon our combined forty years of counseling experience, we feel that thirty days is a realistic time to get your marriage on the right track: to rekindle the feeling that your marriage is positive and loving, to re-establish the perception of your relationship as a partnership rather than a struggle, and to absorb the principles and skills of an effective relationship.

This book is divided into thirty short chapters, each ending in an exercise with a special purpose. Some have been conceived to promote insights or demonstrate specific principles, others to help you acquire necessary skills. Almost all are designed to encourage you to perceive your relationship in ways you possibly haven't considered before. We refer to this as **reframing.**

Every assignment is numbered according to a thirty-day schedule. Take sufficient time to complete each assignment and avoid doing the exercises out of sequence. If you feel that you have not had sufficient time to adequately complete an assignment, *do not move on.* Take an extra day or two. Each assignment is built upon a foundation composed of the previous exercises. This is not a contest to see if you can beat the record for the quickest improvement in a marriage. It is not a failure or a setback if it takes you fifty days or even longer to complete the program.

Some of the exercises prescribed take only a few minutes to complete and require no specific followup. Others, especially those designed to acquire certain skills, are easy enough to complete, but then require constant diligence and practice if you expect to maintain a reasonable level of proficiency. Complete each of the assignments to the best of your ability. At the same time, tune in to any feelings the exercises stir within you. Some of these exercises may make you feel anxious or uncomfortable. That is okay. A little discomfort often goes along with stretching and growing.

As you progress through the book you will likely find that some of the exercises seem less relevant to your marriage than others. Complete those as conscientiously as you do the rest. Assignments that may not seem especially meaningful when you initially read them may ultimately have a significant impact on your relationship.

We strongly suggest that you take notes. It probably would be best if you kept them in a small notebook, so that it will be easier to reflect on your feelings later.

Do not attempt any shortcuts and do not discontinue the program even if your relationship significantly improves in less than thirty days. Behavioral changes can happen quickly, but internal changes often take considerably longer. If your relationship feels as if it is deteriorating, do not discontinue the program. Frequently when communication skills improve and more issues are brought into the open, the change can feel like a jolt to the relationship. Continue reading the book and conscientiously work until you have completed all of the assignments.

For some people change is exciting, while for others it can be extremely frightening. The reality is that all people change and all relationships evolve. Our goal is to help you be an agent for change in your relationship rather than a victim of outside changes. If your goal has been to hold on to the past and try to slow the pace of change, then the concepts and assignments contained in this book may be frightening. If that is the case, read through this entire book carefully, without doing any of the exercises. When you have finished, go back to the beginning, and start each assignment only when you are ready.

You and your mate are each unique individuals with distinct feelings, thoughts, and needs. Because you have joined hands in matrimony does not mean that either of you must surrender your individuality. Consequently, you will not find any formulas in this book for how your marriage ought to be. Rather, this book will help you explore and pursue **your own** wants, feelings, and goals and provide you with the tools and the skills to forge a progressive and fulfilling relationship.

We offer no magic formula to eliminate all the stress from your marriage. At the very least you will have to weather the normal crises that all of us face as the result of ongoing developmental changes: aging, career choices, births and deaths, and so on. Our goal is to help you achieve consistent growth and improvement, not perfection.

## DAY 1

# *Marital Change*

You are a different person than you were when you first married, and so is your spouse. Both of you have changed, as has your relationship. Even if you struggle to keep your world constant, it changes: jobs change, roles change, and so does your relationship. You move; your children grow; the lines on your face deepen. We are all participants in and, to some extent, victims of a changing environment. There is no way to inhibit the tide of change. Your life is a dynamic system, constantly moving and adjusting. It is not a matter of *whether* you choose to change, only a matter of *how* you do it. And often that is not a matter of choice.

Every change in your life has some effect on your marriage. Major changes, like getting a new job, having a child, or moving to a new location, have obvious and often immediate effects. But change is also a consequence of much less notable events: the warm feelings you absorb every time you receive a genuine gesture of love or the sense of loss when affections you take for granted are omitted.

Virtually everything your mate does has an effect on

5

you, and likewise, your actions have considerable impact on your spouse and on your relationship. Your behavior and your partner's are inseparably intertwined, often in unpredictable ways, but nonetheless, they are linked.

Unlike traditional marriage counseling and virtually all other techniques to aid your marriage, the thirty-day program in this book does not require your partner's involvement. This is a book **for you,** not for you **and** your partner.

Whether your partner has been satisfied with the status quo, is too stubborn to change, or is too busy to be involved, you will be able to alter your marriage. Even if the two of you have been willing to try but have not known what steps to take, this thirty-day program will still empower you to bring change to your relationship. The exercises provided will not bestow upon you any magical or mysterious capacity, but they will help you recognize a strength you have always possessed, assist you in mobilizing it, and teach you the skills to use it constructively.

Obviously in any relationship change in both partners is essential for the growth of the relationship. And without a doubt, this program will work more effectively if both you and your partner are motivated and open to change. However, trying to directly influence your partner can sometimes intensify a power struggle in the relationship. You are certainly welcome to share your experiences with your spouse, but don't pressure him or her to participate. If your partner is curious about the changes that occur, feel free to talk about them. Whether or not your mate reads the book should have no effect on your successful completion of the program. There are some exercises in the latter part of the book that request your partner's involvement, but even then you still remain the focus of the exercise. In the event that your partner is unwilling to participate, alternative exercises are provided. Do not try to alter his or her decision.

Some people caught in the inevitable differences and struggles of marriage feel like victims. Frequently a person in that situation sees his/her actions as a defensive reflex to an unreasonable or uncaring mate. Therefore, the person assumes that the only hope lies in changing the partner. This is a losing battle. The common fear is: *If I let go, and don't keep after him/her, my partner will never make an effort to change and my marriage will always be as it is now.* Yet the harder one partner pushes, the greater the resistance from the other. The net result is no movement. In one sense a person with that fear might be right. If he or she stops pushing, there **may** be no movement. However, if the person continues to push, there definitely will be no movement. Try the following:

> *Clasp your hands together, keeping your elbows extended outward, and push so that your palms are pressing against each other. Now increase the force with which you push with one arm. Notice that the other arm compensates automatically to push back. There is still no movement.*
>
> *Keep pushing and feel the tension in your arms. Also feel how tiring this can be after just a few minutes.*
>
> *Now, relax one arm, and observe how the tense arm comes over toward the side of the relaxed arm.*

Notice that when you pushed your two hands against each other, there was no movement, and, when you pushed harder with one hand, the other automatically compensated and both became tired from the constant struggle. The only way you were able to bring change to the status quo was for one arm to stop pushing.

This is exactly what happens in marital power struggles. If you try to force your partner into change, you become an active participant in a power struggle. The only solution that has any chance of success is to give up trying to change him or her. You can't have a tug of war with only one team.

Ironically, by putting your energy into trying to dictate your partner's actions you actually end up feeling powerless. Your partner controls his or her own behavior. The only power you possess in a marital conflict is your ability to change yourself. That is what this book is about: changing your own behavior, so you can bring change to your marriage.

As you alter your own behavior over the next thirty days, do not keep score as to how much your mate is changing, or grade whether he or she is changing enough. Many of your partner's changes may be internal and not at all observable. The point of the exercises in this book have nothing to do with manipulating your partner to change.

The simple exercise that follows is designed to demonstrate that any change in your actions will bring notice from your partner, and ultimately will result in a change in his/her behavior. During the next thirty days, you will use this fundamental law of human nature to ignite a chain of events that ultimately can lead to significant improvement in the relationship. There is no doubt—you can change your marriage! This begins Day 1 of your thirty-day program. To paraphrase an old bumper sticker: *This is the first day of the rest of your relationship.*

### EXERCISE 1

Make three changes in your behavioral routine that your partner is likely to notice. Here are just a few of the many possibilities:

- *Walk your partner to the car in the morning and call to say hello during the day.*
- *Make a suggestion to go somewhere together that you don't usually go (like a walk, shopping)*
- *Sit in a different seat than you usually do while the two of you are watching TV (sit closer or sit on the other side of the room)*

Observe and write down any alterations this elicits in your partner's behavior (e.g., strange looks, comments, or questions).

The results of this first assignment are not intended to bring any dramatic change to your relationship. The point of this exercise is that you can change your marriage simply by altering your own behavior. Not necessarily positive change and not necessarily predictable change, just change. **You do have an impact on your relationship.**

# The Ingredients of Constructive Change

Adjusting to the changing tides and building a successful marriage has nothing to do with random luck, chemistry, or intuition. The ability to maintain and grow within any type of relationship involves three key ingredients: skill, motivation, and time.

### Marital Skills

You and your partner already have some skills at carrying on a relationship. Otherwise your marriage would not have developed to its current level. However, if you take a look at how you acquired those skills, you will have your first clue as to why sustaining and improving a marriage can be so complex. Obviously you were not born with the skills to carry on a relationship, nor did you magically acquire them. Those skills were learned. Not through any formalized training, but through a procedure that included observation and a process of trial and error.

It seems ironic. For an uncomplicated task like riding a bicycle you received careful training. Yet no one ever instructed you on the complexities of sustaining a close and intimate relationship. The primary classroom for your marital education was the home you were raised in, and the teachers were your parents. Certainly there were other classrooms and other teachers: you might have learned from relatives, friends, television, movies, books, and many other sources. But the underlying foundation for all of your marital interactions was the parental relationship you observed growing up. Which is not to say that you have tried to imitate your parents. You may even have tried your hardest to avoid carrying on a relationship like theirs. But the fact is that much of what you and your partner have learned in the way of skills, both constructive and destructive, was unconsciously absorbed through your roots. And your parents, like yourself, received their basic schooling in the skills of marriage from their parents.

### Motivation

Motivation is a double-edged sword. Everyone is familiar with relationships that fail or flounder because of a lack of motivation. Obviously, this is not your problem. The fact that you are reading this book indicates you haven't run out of steam yet.

Yet many relationships encounter major problems because one of the partners is "too motivated." He (or she) is so intense about changing the relationship that gradual changes appear insignificant when compared to his zealous expectations. Consequently he becomes frustrated, angry, and critical of his partner's "lack of effort" and ends up sabotaging the very results he desires.

A number of years ago, while we were consulting at

an elementary school, a teacher asked us to help with a student who was constantly calling out to her and interrupting the class. Together we devised a program, and in order to measure its progress, we asked her first to measure how often the child was calling out. She counted 28 times.

She then implemented our program, but three days later she came to us in frustration. "This program isn't working," she said rather emphatically and angrily. The child's behavior was so annoying and upsetting that the teacher was ready to throw in the towel. We asked her to again count the student's interruptions. The following day she counted 23 outbursts. The child was adjusting to her change in behavior, but the difference between a child disrupting a room 23 times a day or 28 times a day was imperceptible. The student seemed just as disruptive.

We suggested that rather than throwing in the towel, she continue the program and mention to the child that she noticed the effort he was making to control himself and how much she appreciated his effort. She did so, and within three weeks the annoying behavior was eliminated.

The point is, if you are looking for swift major changes, you often miss the minor adjustments that evolve into major changes later on.

*Committing Time*

Sooner or later, time causes tension in all our marriages. We live in a society where time is at a premium, and all of us go through periods when we feel absolutely overwhelmed. Often in marriage counseling we hear people claim they are pressed for time. They make commitments to work, children, school, different charitable organizations, etc., and suddenly realize that they can't *find* enough time to devote to their marital relationship.

It is not a matter of whether you can *find* time for your marriage, it is a matter of whether you *choose to make* time for your marriage. If you want to make your relationship work, you must place it as a high priority in your life.

Many of our marriage counseling clients debate this concept when we first present it. They contend that they must work hard to keep up their rent or mortgage payments, that they have commitments to spend time with their children, church, school, etc. They simply don't have enough time to devote to their partners, even though they protest that they would like to. These are all very persuasive arguments, but basically what these individuals are asserting is that their jobs, their children, or their church occupy a higher priority than their marriage. When these clients make the *choice* to spend more time with their spouses, the former commitments are not eliminated, they are simply moved to a lower slot on the list of priorities.

If you have a very crowded schedule, do not rely on spontaneously finding time to spend with your spouse. Many people expect to find time for their partner during the week, only to find that their well-intentioned plans get sidetracked by *more important* obligations or intrusions. If this has been a problem for you, set aside a block of time to be with your spouse for a few hours, once or twice a week, time that will be dedicated to the two of you. If you receive a telephone call during that time, tell the person you will call back (or if you have a phone answering machine, set it to answer your calls). If your children interrupt, tell them this is Mom and Dad's special time, and you want to be left alone.

This may sound very cold, but if you are someone

who is very busy it may be the best possible alternative until you can arrange for more time in your schedule.

If you choose not to spend time with your spouse, do not pretend you are a victim of circumstances. Certainly there are periods of time in our lives when the circumstances force us to focus our attention on other distractions. However, if your relationship is constantly receiving short shrift, the quality of your marriage will pay a serious price.

Consider this program as part of your time commitment to your relationship. To use it effectively you will have to allow about thirty minutes each day. And when you have completed the next twenty-nine exercises, you can use that half-hour to devote to your relationship.

---

### EXERCISE 2

During the next twenty-four hours take a look at how much time you actually spend being with your mate. Then take a look at your activities during that twenty-four-hour period and make a list of what your priorities seemed to have been—including self, marriage, children, parents, job, church, friends, etc.

Example:

1. Job
2. Classwork—finishing my degree at school
3. Spending time with the children
4. Marriage—spending time with my wife
5. Personal recreation

When you have completed your list, rearrange the priorities into the order you would like them to be in. Then write out what changes you will have to make in your life to make that new priority list a reality.

You will not suddenly be able to change your lifestyle. Even if you made the choice to establish your marriage as a higher priority, you would not be able to transform your schedule overnight. For right now, just notice any discrepancy between what you would like your priorities to be, and what they actually are.

When you do choose to make a change, recognize that it will take months. Complete prior commitments, but be cautious before assuming any new ones. Be especially conscious of taking on new responsibilities to work overtime, join committees, take classes, etc. Even be aware before adding any additional family commitments. Time with your family is also necessary in a relationship, but it is not the same as setting aside time for your marriage.

# The Kaleidoscope of Marriage

Your view of reality is distorted. Your perception of your partner is distorted. How you perceive your children and your parents is distorted, and even your view of yourself is distorted. In fact, everything you see, say, hear, and feel has an element of distortion.

Take for example these two lines:

―――――――――――――――――――――――――

―――――――――――――――――――――――――

As you look at these lines, your eyes, unburdened by any other influences, easily compare the two and your brain correctly determines that they are the same length. However, if the same lines are placed in the context of a different **frame of reference** your eyes evaluate the length of the lines, but your mind cannot separate the horizontal lines from the cues surrounding them:

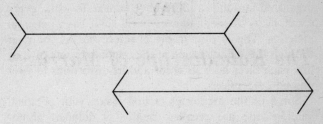

Your conclusion is distorted. Even though the two horizontal lines are of equal length, your **personal reality** at this moment is that the line on top appears to be longer than the one underneath. Your perception of the two horizontal lines is influenced by the context in which they occur.

### Frame of Reference

All your perceptions in life are affected by their frame of reference. Go into a quiet room and drop a pin. Your ears clearly hear the sound of the pin hitting the floor. Now go into the bathroom, turn on the bath water, and drop the same pin on the floor. The pin makes just as loud a noise as it hits the ground, but the background noise masks the sound. You never hear it.

When it comes to life experiences your frame of reference is much more complex than those just illustrated. In a sense, your personal perceptions are a series of illusions—perceptions distorted by all the biological, historical, and emotional factors that make you a unique individual. Your lifetime has been a continuum of events, and every one is now a part of your frame of reference.

Imagine that all the events of your rich history were recorded on colorful layers in a kaleidoscope, each layer organized around a different theme. To you, every event, every theme, and every vivid color has a personal meaning. This is your frame of reference. As you peer through this kaleidoscope at the ongoing events of your life, each layer adds its color and its distortions to your unique perceptions.

Some of the memories etched inside your personal kaleidoscope are recalled clearly as detailed photographs while others have eroded over time, their clarity faded into vague recollections or rewritten as romanticized fiction or frightful nightmares. Yet, all have become part of your frame of reference: layers of memories, some sharp, some fuzzy. Every person and every event throughout your life has colored your expectations about marriage, marital partners, and every other aspect of living, resulting in a unique personal reality. Even your most recent experience, reading this page, has become a part of your frame of reference and may influence your future behavior.

Everything you experience in life is viewed through this unique kaleidoscope. Your personal reality is unlike that of any other human being. Every event is subject to a personal interpretation: every perception you have of your spouse and every image of yourself; every event you have participated in and will participate in; everything you see and everything you hear.

Look at any object or concept: something as concrete as a tree, or as intangible as the memory of an event that occurred years ago. It doesn't really matter what the object or concept is that you are considering, we will call it **X**: the object as it actually exists before any interpretation.

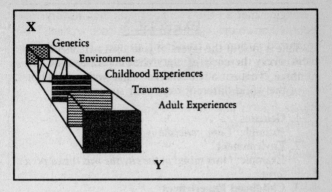

When you look at **X** you view it through your own unique frame of reference. As the image of the event is filtered through the layers of your kaleidoscope, all the events of your life, divided into themes, add an element of distortion to your perception. There is a gender layer, which has to do with being male or female, another having to do with how your parents treated you, and still other layers with themes about the environment in which you were raised, your childhood experiences, your medical history, your various relationships, the way you feel at the moment, and so on. By the time the light of your perception has filtered through this infinity of layers, you have added considerable distortion and bias to your perception of **X**. What you see is **Y**. This is your personal reality.

Because you have looked through the same kaleidoscope your whole life, you are completely unaware of its influence. It is like looking through a pair of sunglasses: after your eyes become accustomed to the different level of light filtering through, you forget that the glasses are there.

---

### EXERCISE 3

Take a look at the layers of your own personal kaleidoscope. In each of the following categories, list three events or attributes that make your perception of the world different from your spouse's.

1. **Genetics**
   Example: *I am male/she is female.*
2. **Environment**
   Example: *I was raised in the city/she was raised on a farm.*
3. **Childhood Experiences**
   Example: *I was encouraged to be athletic/she was told she was uncoordinated.*
4. **Traumas**
   Example: *I was physically abused as a child/she was not.*
5. **Adult Experiences**
   Example: *I had a wife who left me for another man/ she chose to leave her former husband.*

---

Your perspective is completely different from your marital partner's, biased by a dissimilar set of life experiences. The two of you are of different backgrounds, of different parents. Each of you has lived in different environments and has a different biological makeup. Each is a unique individual, different from anyone else who has ever lived, perceiving life through a unique kaleidoscope. It is not possible for the two of you to see the world exactly alike.

# *Marital Pioneering*

The world has gone through a technological, social, and economic revolution. Since the turn of the century, we have added twenty years to the average lifespan and decreased the size of the average household from five persons to three. We have progressed from an age of lumbering locomotives and primitive automobiles to one in which commercial jets span the world in hours and manmade satellites explore the outer reaches of our solar system. Ours world is a jet-paced society that offers an unending number of options. We are a society of contrasts. At times a violent "I"-oriented and dog-eat-dog mass, at other times a community of peaceful and supportive nurturers. Ours is a global culture that peers into other societies through an electronic window and then attempts to assimilate an assortment of heterogeneous values.

### *Changing Roles*

The previously accepted norms of the self-sacrificing female and the dominating male have been replaced by a continuum of overlapping roles. The covert premise of intellectual and social inequality between the sexes is gradually being replaced by a new spirit of equality. At the turn of the century only 18.8 percent of women worked, as opposed to 57.5 percent in 1990. Today, women compete equally in the workplace and have assumed roles as captains of industry that were unimaginable to our grandparents. It is now acceptable and even expected that women be open and assertive. For men, vulnerability and expression of feelings are also allowed and even encouraged, as is active participation in child-rearing and day-to-day household chores. Rigidity and scarcity of options have given way to a tolerance for a wide range of ideas, lifestyles, and beliefs. *Individuality, open communication,* and *self-development* have become our new buzzwords.

For our grandparents, and even for many of our parents, life was contained within the confines of a relatively stable, unchanging, slow-paced society where the concept of *family* had a special meaning. There was *family,* and then there was the rest of the world. The family was a closely tied unit that included everyone; even distantly related cousins, second cousins, and aunts twice removed. Often they lived in close proximity, sharing similar religious beliefs, ethnic customs, and values. The geographic intimacy of family members alone was sufficient to influence the decisions and values of others in the clan.

Options were few for our forefathers, and their marriages reflected that. Alternatives for marriage were clearly limited. As individuals, they were expected to choose a mate who shared a similar background and beliefs and continue to conform to the values and wishes of the family. This preserved the homogeneity of the family and allowed it to remain as an intact unit.

In a sense, virtually all of us begin our marriages in

the shadow of what is often referred to as the "traditional marriage": a nostalgic resurrection of the marital values of our forefathers. Whether we embrace its assumptions and basic structure or we completely reject its underlying philosophy and goals, we have been influenced by the traditional marriage. It promises a simpler and more secure relationship but the reality of this model is quite different than the commonly held fantasy.

We have been told that the traditional marriage is a family-oriented model with well-defined roles. The man acts as the head of the household, works, makes the major life decisions, and is the financially responsible partner while his wife tirelessly and happily takes care of the children and the home. Her basic job is to subordinate her needs to that of her husband and the family. If all goes according to the script, the children are obedient and loving. It is a safe and secure system in which everyone knows and readily accepts his or her role, and both partners enjoy a pressure-free marriage.

This perception of marriage is further romanticized by the exaggerated images we see portrayed in television and movies, as well as the more subtle influences of the advertising media.

> *The contemporary woman wants just what her mother wanted: a home, husband, and children. She may also want a job, but it is just something to supplement the family income, not an encompassing career that could keep her working late at the office. She has realized . . . that being a wife can be fun—I don't need anything else.* *

> *My mother was convinced the center of the world was 36 Maplewood Drive. Her idea of a wonderful time was*

---

* *Los Angeles Times,* 26 December 1988, section V, p. 1.

*Sunday dinner. She bought UNICEF cards, but what really mattered were the Girl Scouts. And she felt, no matter what, there was always enough love to go around. . . . The finest cherished things in my mother's life were her husband, her children, and the wedding china she never dared to use.*\*\*

Regardless of whether the traditional marriage is an accurate replication of what our forefathers experienced or just a colorful fantasy, it is probably the cultural cornerstone upon which your marital frame of reference is built. Society has changed drastically, as have the skills that are necessary to adapt to those radical differences, but your fantasies and ideals about marriage have been indelibly influenced by a notion born in a different era.

### Marital Pioneering

You are a unique person in a unique relationship with a unique partner, and you live in a unique society at a unique point in history. Your relationship is unlike any that ever was, or ever will be. Yet, even though you perceive your marriage through a distinct frame of reference, some of the tools you use are still antiquated hand-me-downs evolved from the relationship model of your parents; tools based upon two frames of reference that are vastly different than your own.

The frame of reference offered to us by our parents no longer fits. Today, newly coined sociological terms such as *extended family, family of origin, nuclear family, fractured family,* and *single-parent family* reflect the increased risk to the family unit as our parents or grandparents knew it. Frequently, families become spread all over the globe and weekly or monthly telephone calls

\*\* *Good Housekeeping* radio spot, quoted in *Los Angeles Times,* 26 December 1988, section V, p. 1.

replace face-to-face conversation as a mode of intimacy. Family visits often are relegated to annual events rather than part of the daily or weekly routine.

It is arguable whether the quality of life is better now than at the turn of the century, but there can be no argument that our lives are very different. This is not a judgment that the traditional marriage ought to be extinct. Certainly, in its most rigid form, it is a dinosaur that is somewhat ill-adapted to many of the dynamic tides that affect most of our lives. What is a problem, however, is that many couples initially assume the sanctity of this traditional model when they enter into a marriage, only to have their romanticized fantasies dashed by the reality of a modern culture.

You are a marital pioneer, blazing new and unique trails through the wilderness of 1990s relationships, yet your frame of reference has been warped by outdated concepts and assumptions spawned by previous generations. If your marriage is to survive, it must have the agility to borrow from the older more traditional model yet adapt to an innovative model that would have been unimaginable for our parents.

This exercise will give you some idea of the powerful role that your background plays in determining your values and perceptions.

---

### EXERCISE 4

Look through a couple of magazines and find a picture of a setting that you find ideal—maybe a tropical paradise, or a foreign city. Now find a picture of yourself as a child, and place the picture of you next to the one in the magazine. Imagine yourself being raised in this setting and how it might have changed
*Continued*

your outlook on the type of car you drive, the type of neighborhood you now live in, and the type of partner you chose to marry.

When that is completed, find another picture in the magazine and repeat the exercise.

# *Personal Expectations*

As a result of all the events throughout your life you have formed a series of expectations. You have expectations about men, about women, about your own capabilities, about your partner, and about virtually every other topic imaginable. And every one of those expectations affects your perceptions. Take, for example, something as simple as your expectations of the printing on this page. Look at the following illustration:

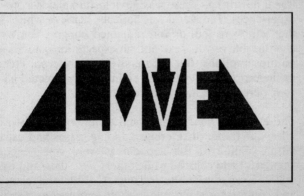

Most likely, your initial impression is that you are looking at some figures that resemble ancient hieroglyphics. Your brain organizes according to what it expects to see: black figures on a white background. After all, that is how this book is printed: black letters on white pages. However, if you reverse that expectation, and instead, allow yourself to see white letters on a black background, you will see the word *LOVE*. If you have difficulty seeing this, hold the book farther away. If you still can't read it, turn to appendix B at the end of this book. You will see the same figure with two lines added. Interestingly, once you are able to see the world *LOVE,* your expectation is changed, and it is hard **not** to see it when you look at it again.

Similarly, your marital relationship is strongly influenced by your expectations. Based upon the colors of your past experiences, you entered your marriage as a breathing mass of biases, beliefs, and expectations.

When you were born, your basic needs were instinctive: eating, sleeping, drinking, physical warmth, and emotional nurturing. There was no colorful kaleidoscope of experiences. The world was basically black or white. Either you were fed, or you remained hungry. You were comfortable or you were not; no expectations, no biases, no presumptions. But progressively, every event etched its fingerprint onto your life and indelibly affected all of your perceptions and your relationships.

The events of your infancy and childhood were woven into your frame of reference, adding biases and expectations. Some of the happenings were conspicuously wonderful and colorful while others were dark and traumatic. Even the subtle innuendos, disdainful glances, and comforting smiles made their impressions. Gradually, you learned to distinguish those faces which brought nurturing from those that disappointed, and all of those visages became a part of your kaleidoscope.

Every action of your father's and every movement by your mother etched a picture of how men and women act. Every time you saw your parents embrace and every time you saw them argue, an image was emblazoned in your mind about men, women, and committed relationships. Whether your parents totally immersed themselves in your life or were virtually absent, whether they were supportive or unavailable, their influence indelibly marked your perceptions of yourself, your mate, and your marital relationship.

The actions and inactions of your parents were contrasted against what you viewed in the homes of your friends, and again your expectations were altered. Fictional sources such as fairy tales, novels, TV, movies, and even advertisements, further influenced your impressions. Gradually childhood blended into adolescence and adolescence gave way to adulthood; every event and every relationship adding to your frame of reference.

Every one of your life experiences influenced your dreams and expectations of what your Prince or Princess Charming would be like. Those expectations formed a frame around what you saw when you finally met your present partner. If you expected to see a saint, you may have whitewashed some of your partner's shortcomings and seen them as assets. If you expected a snake, you may have done just the opposite.

The following case history demonstrates how two people in a relationship can distort reality based upon their personal frame of reference. When reading through this history, please note that neither person is wrong. Both color the incident in accordance with their own expectations and prior experiences.

*Jennifer was all set to take her licensing exam to become a psychologist. Since the exam was early Monday morning and was given more than a hundred miles from their home, she and Tom decided to spend the weekend in the city the exam was given. They hoped this would reduce the tension that had filled their home for the past six months while Jennifer studied. While Tom checked into the hotel, Jennifer disappeared to make a few phone calls. As part of the check-in procedure, Tom was asked whether he preferred a smoking or non-smoking room, and he made what seemed like an easy decision. Since he didn't smoke, and Jennifer had recently given up smoking, he arranged for a non-smoking room. When he completed the check-in and told Jennifer, she was furious.*

*Jennifer felt as though he was being controlling and manipulative by making sure she didn't smoke. She had often felt that Tom's behavior was manipulative and controlling in much the same way as she viewed her parents. His actions at the hotel simply reiterated her beliefs. She found it impossible to believe that he chose the room to be supportive of her non-smoking. Her instinctive response to Tom, or anyone else she perceived as manipulative or controlling, was to act rebellious.*

*Tom's frame of reference was quite different. He had always felt intimidated by Jennifer's anger. Therefore, he avoided confrontations. Rather than being direct, Tom would frequently try to manipulate or coerce Jennifer into viewing things his way. This was the way his parents had communicated with each other. However, this time he truly felt he was being supportive by choosing a non-smoking room. In addition, since she had been critical of him in the past for not making decisions, he felt as if*

*he needed to make the decision without her input. He
didn't want to risk an argument, especially because he
knew she was already tense because of the exam.*

Both of Jennifer and Tom's histories and backgrounds
became integral to determining how this argument escalated. Although, for some couples choosing a non-smoking room might have been seen as a minor issue, for
Jennifer and Tom it brought their marriage to the brink
of disaster.

### Personal Interpretation

Even in the simplest of personal interactions, a great
deal of interpretation takes place. Like a computer processing a pile of data, your mind instantaneously ana-
lyzes the literal meaning of the words it hears, the
context in which they are said, and the tone of voice,
facial expressions, and every body movement of the person who is communicating with you. Then, in a fraction
of a second, it interprets this complex data, discerns a
meaning, and you respond.

It is difficult to recognize how much interpretation
your mind does, and how quickly it does it, until you are
faced with communication that occurs without this in-
terpretive step. A delightful example of this occurs in a
series of children's stories about Amelia Bedelia, written by Peggy Parish. Amelia is a maid who interprets
everything literally. Because she responds to the words,
and does not interpret the intent, even the simplest
verbalization gets miscommunicated. In one book,
Amelia Bedelia is assigned a list of chores to complete,
including one which reads: *Dust the furniture.*

After reading the instructions she responds:
  "Did you ever hear tell of such a thing.

At my house we undust the furniture. But each to his own way."

Amelia Bedelia took one last look at the bathroom.
She saw a big box with the words *Dusting Powder* on it.
"Well, look at that.
A special powder to dust with!" exclaimed Amelia Bedelia.

So Amelia Bedelia dusted the furniture.
"That should be dusty enough.
How nice it smells."

There will always be some degree of distortion in every action you take. Even though you like to think of yourself as objective, that is an impossibility. You can never rid yourself of the frame of reference formed by your background experiences, nor can you neutralize the effects of your expectations, desires, dreams, and biases. They are a part of your life, and they play an important role in your marriage.

---

### EXERCISE 5

Fold a piece of paper in half and on one side write down three personality traits about your partner you would like changed.
    Example:

1. *Stubborn*
2. *Talks too much*
3. *Obsesses about money*

Now, find a picture of your partner that you really like, from early in your relationship or a time you were getting along very well. Look at the picture for a couple of moments and recall what your relationship was like then. Think in particular about the three traits you have written down. No doubt they existed then, but chances are you framed them differently.

On the other side of the paper, write how you viewed those traits at the time the picture was taken. Example:

1. *Stubborn—Strong-willed, stands up for what he believes*
2. *Talks too much—Sociable, meets people easily*
3. *Obsesses about money—Generous, showers me with gifts*

Which is accurate, your perception of your partner when you first met or the one you hold now? Both are distortions based upon your personal frame of reference at the time. You distorted then, based upon one set of expectations, and you distort now, based upon another set.

## DAY 6

# *Weighted Distortions*

Not all the events of your life play an equally important role in distorting your perception. Both triumphs and traumas play a prominent role in coloring your perceptions. Any event that causes you severe emotional or physical pain or any that results in noticeable comfort and nurturing will become an integral part of your kaleidoscope. Of special importance in coloring your perceptions will be such traumas as deaths, divorces, serious illnesses, loss of pets, moving, and physical or emotional abuse.

Abuse is not something that just happens to other people. In one form or another, all of us have experienced abuse during our lifetime. Abuse is any act inflicted by one person that maligns the dignity of another. Any behavior that hurts, provokes, intimidates, coerces, retaliates, or demeans is a form of abuse. It can be physical or verbal, conscious or unconscious, or a defensive reflex. In its most recognizable forms it is seen as physical violence, inappropriate sexual contact, or verbal threats. Other times it may be more insidious, assuming such forms as criticism, intimidation, demeaning remarks, neglect, or judgment. It may consist of a single traumatizing event that occurs in a matter of seconds or minutes, or it can take on a more subtle form and occur over a period of years. Often the abuse is portrayed under the guise of love or caring.

*Joseph brought to therapy a memory from when he was six. At that age he had two cats, both of which he loved, but which he felt were being mistreated by his father. Repeatedly he tried to teach the cats how to run away from home so that they would have a better environment. Unfortunately, during one of these episodes, one of his cats was run over and killed. The trauma of this single event followed Joseph into his adulthood. It colored not only his view of pets, but more important, it affected his relationship with women. He felt responsible for killing something he dearly loved. He was afraid of getting close because he was afraid he would feel the pain of grieving a loss. It became a self-fulfilling prophecy. He kept women at a distance and, inevitably, they would leave him. Every loss became a part of his history and made intimacy with others even less likely.*

*This single event was not solely responsible for his avoidance of intimacy. His father was emotionally abusive, and Joseph felt that his mother never properly protected him. It was he who really wanted to run away from home. Both the single incident of his cat being killed and the longer-term abuse and neglect that he felt from his parents damaged his ability to trust and distorted his perception of intimacy.*

Whatever the nature of the abuse or the time frame within which it occurs, no matter how obvious or subtle, or under whatever guise it is implemented, abuse is abuse. In fact, there has been some speculation among mental health professionals that subtle or well-disguised forms of emotional abuse may be more durable and destructive than the most obvious forms of physical abuse. They hypothesize that survivors of overtly abusive situations are able to neutralize some of the negative effects of their abusive past by understanding the "crazy" nature of their abusers. On the other hand, those who have been subtly abused or neglected often do not realize that there was anything dysfunctional in the treatment they received. Consequently, they treat others in the same abusive way they were treated. Contrast the following two histories:

*Tina was abused as a child. Her alcoholic mother hit her, kicked her, and constantly demeaned Tina with awful accusations and disparaging remarks. Rarely did the mother display any affection. Tina's father abandoned her when she was born, and her mother remarried a man who sexually abused Tina. From age seven, Tina could tell that she was treated differently than her friends. She knew she was abused, but she blamed it on herself. She imagined that if she only could be a better daughter, she would be treated like others.*

*By the time she reached her teens, Tina could look back and identify herself as an abused child. Although she still blamed herself, she knew that the actions of her mother and stepfather were "crazy." At that point, she made a conscious choice not to be like her mother. By the time she was twenty-two, she was married for the second time and had two children. She knew she did not want her children to have a childhood like her own. Like her mother, Tina was an alcoholic, but unlike her mother, Tina realized she needed help. She joined Alcoholics Anonymous, and as soon as she could afford it, she entered therapy. Twice over a period of ten years she initialized hospitalizations for herself, once to deal with her alcoholism and another time to deal with her abuse. She also discovered religion as a way of comforting herself. She worked for fifteen years at one job to regain her pride and confidence and then went to college at age thirty-five to give herself the financial foundation she needed to build a new life. Because she knew that her own background was abusive, she was able to make the changes necessary to give her husband and her children what she had been deprived of: a loving home without the constant threat of abuse.*

*Norma came from a family with two parents who loved her. Neither parent was alcoholic and neither one was overtly abusive. However, her father could not hold down a job and her mother worked up to twelve hours a day, six days a week, to keep the family afloat. Her father was rarely at home. Neither parent had time for the children, but on the rare occasions they did, they squandered the time by bickering between themselves.*

*With no parents at home, Norma was left to be a parent to the three younger children. From age seven she had to deal with every crisis. She had to make the daily household decisions, and she had to comfort her brothers and sister. There was no adult at home to comfort Norma. She was scared and lonely in her parental role and knew nothing about having fun like other children.*

*As an adult Norma married a man who worked diligently and earned enough so she could remain at home to raise the children. But, when it came to giving physical or emotional attention to her children or husband, Norma did not have a clue as to what to do. She encouraged her husband in his work, and with the fruits of his labor bought the children the physical comforts in life—a beautiful home, clothing, and so forth. However, Norma had no idea how to nurture her children or give them emotional warmth. Norma had not been abused in the traditional sense, but because her neglect as a*

*child had been so subtle, she never knew that she had
lacked anything as a child. Consequently, Norma did
not even realize that her children were deprived of physical and emotional affection. She could not give what
she never knew she was lacking.*

For both Tina and Norma, the past strongly affected
their perceptions and influenced the direction of their
lives. They lived what they learned.

The exercise at the end of this chapter and some of
the other assignments in this book are intended to be
adventures to help you connect your present perceptions with your historical past. Some of the memories
the exercises elicit will, we hope, be joyous, interesting,
and wonderful. However, as with any adventure, there
are risks. Some memories may involve painful wounds
that have lain dormant or subconscious. Our hope is
that by exploring these disturbing memories and gaining
insight, healing will begin. However, if the injuries are
too deep, the simple salves offered by this book will not
be sufficient to complete the process of healing. Consequently, as you proceed through each assignment, if the
material that you get in touch with is very painful,
frightening, or overwhelming, feel free to either discontinue the exercise or to at least take a break. Write down
your feelings and thoughts and share them with your
partner or a trusted friend. If the painful memories per-
sist and are disruptive to you, we suggest that you seek
counseling.

If you are already aware that you have some unset-
tling memories about your past and feel that further
digging would be too painful, continue to read the text
in this chapter, but do not participate in the exercise at
the end of this chapter. You already are painfully aware
that your past colors your present. It would be beyond
the scope of this book to point out the painful specifics

to you. However, do not delude yourself by pretending that the influence of these painful memories has faded simply because you have buried them. The effect of these traumatic events will continue to intrude into your perceptions and actions until they are successfully resolved. It is essential that you learn how to use your painful recollections as a way of understanding yourself and your relationships, rather than trying to delete them from your memory. Many excellent therapists, counselors, and support groups are available to help you explore these memories in a constructive way. Day 29 provides direction as to how to find a counselor.

The exercise that follows is designed to help you choose a few of the elements and themes that highlight your frame of reference and give you further insight into how they color and distort your marital relationship. This will help you understand the degree of distortion through which you view yourself and your marriage.

---

### EXERCISE 6

Gather the following materials: a pair of scissors, paste or glue for use on paper, and a piece of construction paper, lightweight cardboard, or a plain piece of paper (in that order or preference) at least 8″-by-10″ and no larger than 16″-by-20″. You will also need to gather two to five magazines (preferably magazines with lots of different pictures).

Flip through the magazines and cut out any pictures, phrases, colors, images, symbols, or anything else that reminds you of your childhood. When you feel you have enough material, paste the clippings to your sheet of paper, so that they form a collage.

Notice each of the items you have chosen. Write
*Continued*

down how you think any of these pictures, phrases, or colors might have relevance to your current relationship.

More than likely what will become apparent from this exercise is that your style of interaction with your partner was significantly influenced by past events and by specific people whom you observed while you were maturing. And that some of those incidents and models were much more instrumental in your development than others.

# Marital Boundaries

Your need for safety is instinctive. If you are physically attacked, your body automatically goes into a protective mode. You might attempt to fight back or you might curl up into a ball, but in one way or another you protect yourself. If you feel attacked verbally, your mind will act to shield you. Like an adept master of the martial arts, your brain reflexively tries to find a way to fend off the attacker and insulate you from harm. But responding to attack after the fact is not always the best way to ensure your personal security. Consequently, sometimes your mind anticipates a physical or emotional invasion, and protectively invokes a series of defensive measures.

### Personal Boundaries

Imagine how vulnerable you would feel living in a home without any walls. Walls define your space, and provide a barrier to protect you. Sooner or later, someone would no doubt read an absence of walls as an open invitation to exploit your vulnerability and to ransack your personal belongings. Your physical safety would be jeopardized. Similarly, to keep others from invading your body, your possessions, or your emotional space, it is necessary to establish physical and emotional borders. These **personal boundaries,** which are drawn by your words or actions, define your space and provide you with protection.

Boundaries come in all sizes and shapes. Some, like medieval fortresses, are built to keep intruders out. Others, like a line of chalk marked on the pavement, are used only to delineate an area and offer no real protection. The bars on a jail cell are designed to contain, while still other boundaries, like a door, are designed to be flexible—to keep some people out, but to let others in.

Along with the advantages of each of these barriers come some disadvantages. To build a great wall and maintain it takes a lot of energy and tends to keep out everyone, those who come in peace as well as those who come in war. A porous boundary, like a line, can feel very vulnerable unless you feel you have the necessary resources to defend it. Walls that keep people in are often resented by the person who is entrapped. And flexible walls work well only if you correctly assess the character of the people you let in as well as those you lock out.

Look around you and notice how every boundary within your line of sight is designed with a specific purpose in mind. Every aspect of the walls, doors, and windows around you was purposely crafted: the dimensions, the weight, the density, and the opaqueness or transparency of materials all serve specific purposes. Notice also that many types of materials are necessary as boundaries in your home, because each serves a different function. No one type of boundary could serve all your purposes.

Similarly, every aspect of your personal boundaries has been engineered with a purpose in mind. Some people, accustomed to betrayal or invasions, find the thought of safety and trust within a relationship to be completely alien. They learn to build impenetrable fortresses to keep everyone out. Others, afraid of rejection and reluctant to scare anyone off, construct barriers that are so porous they are easily permeated. Some people build flexible walls that change depending upon the situation, while others rigidly encapsulate themselves with little regard to circumstances. The type of boundaries you implement will depend upon who and what you are protecting yourself against, how vulnerable you feel, and your own signature pattern of protection established over your lifetime.

Most likely the initial design for your boundaries was conceived during your childhood and has been modified as dictated by circumstances throughout your life. Even the materials that make up your present boundaries—the words you use, how much you smile or frown, your tendency to be direct or indirect, your tone of voice, the way you dress, etc.—were dictated a long time ago. Consequently, some of your boundaries may be out of synch with your adult needs.

If an object comes hurtling at you, you reflexively put your hand up in a gesture of self-protection or move out of the way. Similarly, there are many times during a marriage when simple lines do not feel sufficient to protect you, and your mind and body instinctively erect protective barriers. Most likely you are not conscious of the fact that you have constructed these walls, or if you are aware, you view these barriers as a justifiable consequence of your partner's actions. These may be walls that were established as a result of abuse or deprivation during childhood or previous relationships, or as a reaction to your present marriage. No matter what the underlying reason is, there is no need for you to justify this protective action. In every marital conflict both you and your spouse will react instinctively and do whatever is necessary to protect yourselves.

I LIVE INSIDE A SHELL

THAT IS INSIDE A WALL

THAT IS INSIDE
A FORT

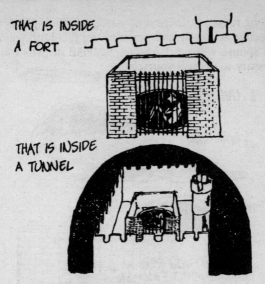

THAT IS INSIDE
A TUNNEL

THAT IS UNDER THE SEA

The following exercise is designed to help you to become aware of the walls you have built. Do the exercise by yourself. As you complete this exercise we encourage you to make notes in your notebook.

---

### EXERCISE 7

The following are examples of barriers people commonly erect. Some of these may sound familiar to you, but more than likely your repertoire will include additional maneuvers not included on this list.

- *Working late at night or finding meetings to attend so that you can regularly be out of the home*
- *Watching TV programs so that you don't have to interact*
- *Acting angry or sarcastic with your partner so that he or she does not attempt to approach you*
- *Going to bed before your partner in order to avoid any physical intimacy*
- *Not talking with, or physically avoiding your partner*
- *Picking at or putting down your partner*

Examine any walls you have erected between you and your partner. Choose one of the walls that you use frequently, and build it even higher. Notice the results. After the twenty-four hours is over you can return the wall to its normal state.

Do not do anything to dismantle your walls at this time. You have erected those defenses as a protective barrier. To suddenly tear them down will likely lead to a feeling of vulnerability, with the natural consequence that you will eventually build them even higher. For now, just make yourself aware of when

*Continued*

and how you erect these barriers. Later, if you gain
some degree of trust and safety, you can choose
whether or not gradually to relax them.

As you complete the above exercise, do not focus
your attention on your partner's barriers. Certainly he
or she has erected similar defenses, but that is not relevant at this time. The purpose of this exercise is to help
you recognize your participation in your marital struggles and to underline the fact that every wall you erect
acts both as a shield and a barrier.

## DAY 8

# Defining Boundaries and Identifying Feelings

Walls and barriers are not the only types of boundaries available. It is a lot easier and takes much less energy to draw a line than to erect a fortress. Likewise, when it comes to making changes, lines are much more flexible than rigid walls. Consequently, setting verbal limits, sharing feelings, and stating what you want in your relationship are preferable to erecting walls and creating distance.

A parable tells the story of a foolish man who, learning that Buddha observed the principle of returning good for evil, came to abuse him. Buddha was silent until the man finished. Then he asked him, "If I decline to accept a gift made to me, to whom then does the gift belong?" The man answered, "In that case it would still belong to the person who offered it." Buddha replied, "Since I decline to accept your abuse, does it not then belong to you?" The man made no reply and walked away slowly, carrying with him that which he had wished to give to another.

Every time you state what you want, what you don't want, or even convey a mere preference, you are setting a boundary, a limit that says: *This is what I need to feel safe and secure.* Every feeling you express likewise sets a boundary, one that says: *This is an area of vulnerability, I trust that you will not hurt me.* In this way you can establish some control over the closeness or distance you choose to have with your partner.

If setting limits is new to you, be careful not to be premature in narrowing the distance between you and your mate. It is essential that you maintain a feeling of safety and security. The reason many attempts to improve a marriage fail is because at the slightest sign of progress one of the partners lowers his or her protective barrier and attempts to move closer. If the other partner does not reciprocate, it feels like a betrayal. Consequently, the original wall is restored and may even be further reinforced for increased safety. You and your mate have a lifetime to get closer. You will need to feel secure in your relationship before you begin to dismantle your defenses.

You do have needs and wants, and you do have limits beyond which you feel overwhelmed. When you don't define who you are by stating your priorities, your partner can only assume that you don't really care. If you choose not to set clear boundaries you send a loud nonverbal message: *My needs are unimportant, my wants are unimportant, and I am unprotected—do to me whatever you wish.* You are giving up your power and setting yourself up to be a victim.

Some people learn to numb their wants and preferences and react to most choices with "I don't care, what do *you* want?" If that is the message your partner receives, your needs are likely to remain unfulfilled. Consequently, it is critical that you be able to define your wants and your needs. The best barometer you have of whether or not you are getting what you want is your body. Just as your stomach *talks* to you to let you know when you are hungry, sick, or anxious, the rest of your body can also be an excellent tool for feedback. Your body is talking, twenty-four hours a day. The question is: *Are you listening?*

The following exercise is a starting point for you to notice that you are a feeling person. By paying attention to your body, you will get all the feedback you need to begin sorting out your priorities. Then you will be able to share these wants with your partner.

---

### EXERCISE 8

If you have a watch that has an alarm, set it to beep every hour. During the next twenty-four hours, every time the alarm goes off notice any feelings in your body: tension, pain, numbness, pressure, etc. Each time, start at the top of your head and slowly work your way down your body, being attentive to even the slightest of body sensations.

If you don't have a watch with an alarm, take the same inventory every time you open or close a door.

---

Don't worry about interpreting what these body feelings mean, just notice that your body is constantly giving you feedback. As you become more conscious of what your body is conveying to you, you will be able to translate these sensations into emotional states (or what most people commonly refer to as *feelings*).

# Setting Your Boundaries

Once you notice your feelings and needs, the next step is recognizing that you have a right to voice them and to take care of yourself. Some people choose to judge this negatively as selfishness. We prefer to think of it as self-nourishing. Think of what the flight attendant announces on an airplane: *"If you have a child with you, when the oxygen masks drop, first place one mask over your own mouth, and then place one over the child's."* If you are starved for oxygen neither you nor your child will survive. In relationships, it is your responsibility to make sure you are nourished. If you don't, your needs won't be fulfilled, and you will not be able to share with your partner without an undertone of resentment.

Likewise, it is your responsibility to provide for your own safety and security. If your total sense of well-being and empowerment is derived from your mate, then he or she can withdraw that safety net at any time, placing you in an extremely vulnerable position. Only you can empower yourself with a feeling of true safety.

If you have doubts about asking for what you want

and setting limits with your spouse, read the following two statements aloud:

1. *My needs are not important, my wants are unimportant, and I choose to remain unprotected.*
2. *My needs are important, my wants are important, and I am responsible for getting them met.*

Choose which of these two statements you wish to adopt. If you choose the first, acknowledge that it is your choice to allow yourself to be victimized. If you choose the second then you are ready to set your boundaries.

When you communicate your boundaries to your spouse, make a **firm,** and **unambiguous** statement of what you want and then listen for the response. The following marital history illustrates how boundaries that are not set with these criteria in mind inevitably lead to resentment and conflict.

*Randall adored Ann at the beginning of their relationship. He felt lucky to have attracted someone so lively and beautiful. Fearful that he could not hold on to the relationship, he tried to win her approval by giving in to her every whim. He made no demands upon her and hoped that in return for his constant attentiveness, she would bestow a little attention on him. However, as it became apparent to him that he was not high on her priority list, his resentment began to grow.*

*All the attention did not go unnoticed by Ann, but instead of being flattered by it, she felt smothered and patronized. However, Ann too felt unwilling to upset the status quo of the relationship with a challenge, because she felt that his attention confirmed that she was a special person.*

*Inside, Ann was feeling rebellious and resentful, but*

*she did not trust herself or Randall enough to express the feelings openly. Instead she acted flirtatious and seductive around other men. It accomplished everything she wanted: it gave her attention, allowed her to feel attractive, and expressed her rebelliousness and resentment. However, she never openly told Randall what she wanted from him.*

*Likewise, when Ann would flirt or act seductive with other men, Randall would lecture, throw a tantrum, or quiz her. His tirades were an effort to control Ann's behavior rather than to clarify his own needs. Both continued to be resentful, but neither clearly stated what they wanted.*

*Eventually, the relationship deteriorated to the point that Randall moved out of the house and both established new relationships. Interestingly, both continued not to set boundaries in their new relationships. Eventually, both Randall and Ann realized that a change in partners was not the answer to their problems, and they entered counseling together as a couple.*

In this actual case history, neither Randall nor Ann ever made clear what they wanted from each other. They were clear about what they did not want, but Randall never said; *"I feel rejected and abandoned. I need some attention. I would like you to make more time for me and our relationship."*

Likewise, Ann never never expressed her feelings and wants: *"I feel resentful and lonely. I need more attention. I do not feel attractive when I am around you."*

### Assessing and Reassessing Boundaries

Just because you define your boundaries does not mean they will always be respected. Sometimes your partner may respect the limits you set, and other times he or she may not. The purpose for setting boundaries is to ensure a feeling of safety. If you don't define yourself then you leave yourself open to be victimized. Inevitably that will lead to resentment, both toward your spouse and toward yourself. On the other hand, clearly stating your boundaries creates a potential to come into conflict with your partner's needs or wants.

For that reason, the skill with which these limits are set and the subsequent flow of communication between you and your partner will be of critical importance to the survival and success of your relationship. Throughout your marriage, you will need to assess which boundaries need to be reaffirmed, redrawn, reinforced, reduced, or eliminated. The ultimate goal of setting boundaries is not to create distance, but rather trust and intimacy.

The purpose of this exercise is to help you see that even when you don't have strong desires and feelings, you do have preferences.

---

### EXERCISE 9

At the next mealtime write down in your notebook what you would prefer to eat, and compare this against what you do eat.

Look through the movie section of a newspaper and see what movie you would prefer to see if you were to go to a movie today.

Think about what you would really like to be doing at this moment. Do you really want to be reading this book, or would you rather be doing something else?

Notice that there are no right or wrong answers, only preferences.

Now, over the next twenty-four hours, notice any
*Continued*

preferences you have and state them. Next time your spouse asks what restaurant you wish to go to, or what movie you want to see, do not answer *"I don't know"*—make a clear choice, and let him or her know what your preference is.

By beginning to tune in to even the most subtle preferences, it will become known that you do have needs and wants. The only question is how clearly you state them.

## DAY 10

# *Trust*

Intimacy, trust, and your ability to set boundaries are inseparably linked. To be intimate in a relationship requires peeling away your protection and allowing yourself to be vulnerable. However, before you can shed your armor, you must feel secure within your relationship. You must **trust** that your partner will be respectful of your boundaries, or at least that you have the power to enforce them. Without trust there can be no intimacy, and without secure boundaries there can be no trust.

Each of us defines our level of trust by peering through our personal kaleidoscope. At one end of the trust spectrum are those whose lives have been enriched by nurturing and loving experiences. For them, the ability to trust and be intimate often seems relatively easy and comfortable. But for others the ability to trust is a scarce commodity, restricted by the scars left by neglect, rejection, death of a loved one, betrayal, or outright abuse. It does not matter whether their wounds occurred during childhood, in a previous adult relationship, or in their present marriage. Their capability to trust another and to be intimate is impaired.

Sometimes those scars are so deep that unqualified trust is not an option. No matter what their partners do, their motives and honesty are questioned. In such situations, counseling is required to return the balance to some semblance of normality.

Of course, trust is not an all or nothing commodity. We have all learned through personal experience to filter information and evaluate who we trust and under what circumstances we trust them. Many of us have learned, for instance, to be wary of the claims and promises of politicians, because of their reputation for ignoring or even contradicting their initial platforms. Unfortunately our skepticism often generalizes beyond the few dishonest political figures and instead extends to virtually all politicians, including those who have been truthful. This is the nature of trust. Only a few negative instances can engender deep and long-lasting skepticism, which can eventually be generalized to similar situations or to other individuals.

### Violations of Trust

When you feel safe in a relationship, there is little need for anything but basic precautions. On the other hand, if you lack trust you will instinctively act protectively. Trust is the most basic and crucial of all covenants in a relationship. In a sense, it is the foundation upon which all of the other marital contracts are built. If the underlying trust is violated, all other contracts and promises became suspect.

Often when people think of violations of trust within a marriage what immediately comes to mind are such infractions as lying or extramarital affairs. However, the experience of trust extends far beyond these two areas. There are many different types of trust in a relationship.

Following are some experiences that come under the banner of *trust:*

*Trust* to be honest and truthful
*Trust* not to betray or abandon
*Trust* to listen without judgment
*Trust* not to ridicule or shame
*Trust* to provide financial security
*Trust* that love will be unconditional
*Trust* that boundaries will be respected
*Trust* that there will be no physical harm

Even the slightest violation within any of these categories represents a breach of trust and can seriously impair the intimacy and destabilize the relationship. The next exercise will help you evaluate if you have a lack of trust in your relationship, and possibly where it originated.

---

### EXERCISE 10

Find a quiet room, with at least two chairs, in which you will be uninterrupted for at least fifteen minutes. Sit in one chair and pretend that your spouse is in the other. Now, using the list of different types of trust in this chapter, speak to the empty chair and say:

*I trust you to be honest and truthful.*
*I trust that you will not betray or abandon me.*
*I trust that you will . . .*

Go through the whole list, repeating them one at a time, and see how much trust you really have in your
*Continued*

partner. If any of the statements does not ring true, notice where your distrust is coming from. Is the distrust rooted in your childhood or in your adult relationships?

## DAY 11

# *Emotional Intimacy*

Sometimes intimacy is a walk on the beach, sometimes a satisfying sexual experience, other times a resolution of pent-up feelings. Every person has his or her own special memories of intimate situations and everyone has their own personal definition for intimacy. This chapter, however, is about a special kind of intimacy: an ability to share emotionally on a daily basis and, when necessary, to expose your most vulnerable self. We refer to this as **emotional intimacy.**

Your need for intimacy in a relationship is not always constant. Just as you are physically comfortable within a range of temperatures, so do you have a range of intimacy within which you experience personal comfort. Not only is this **zone of comfort** based upon your background and personal experiences, but it is affected by a number of conditional factors, including your level of fatigue, your emotional state, the mood of your partner, work and family pressures, personal health, and your degree of confidence in being able to maintain secure boundaries. Your partner, too, has a zone of comfort for intimacy, one which unfortunately is not necessarily in synch with your own. If your partner's ability to engage in intimacy is considerably less than your need for it, do not interpret this to mean you are an unlovable person. The deficit has to do with his or her capacity to be vulnerable at this point. Having a need for intimacy that is greater or lesser than your mate's is not a reflection that one of you is a superior or an inferior being. It is simply a reflection of personal differences.

The zone of comfort might be easier to visualize if you look at the "intimacy meter" below. The meter is marked on a hypothetical scale from zero to 10. Zero represents complete emotional disengagement and an absence of intimacy, and 10 represents a willingness to engage in total synergism, the ultimate degree of intimacy. The shaded area on the scale marks the range within which Joe and Cindy each felt comfortable with intimacy at the beginning of marriage counseling. As you can see, Joe's comfort range for intimacy was fairly narrow (low of 4/high of 6). Cindy, on the other hand, was comfortable within a much broader range (low of 3/high of 8). Under ordinary circumstances, she could tolerate more distance or more closeness without any emotional consequences.

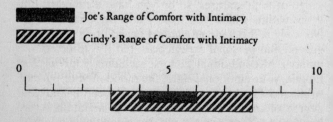

The problem that brought Joe and Cindy into counseling is a common one among couples who experience widely disparate levels in their comfort with intimacy.

As long as their level of intimacy stayed within Joe's comfort range, there were no significant problems. Cindy was also comfortable with that moderate amount of intimacy. However, once the intimacy surpassed Joe's upper limit, he instinctively wanted to reduce the intimacy to a level at which he was comfortable. Cindy, still well within her comfort zone, would crave more. She would try to escalate the level of intimacy by planning special days, being more physically affectionate, and acting more sexually seductive. Joe, on the other hand, would build walls or start a fight to increase the emotional distance and bring the intimacy level down.

A similar pattern would emerge when the intimacy in their relationship was toward the low end of Cindy's comfort level. Joe, feeling uncomfortable with the lack of closeness, would desperately struggle to build more intimacy into the relationship, while Cindy was comfortable with the status quo.

With either scenario, the frustrating tug-of-war would cause the remaining intimacy to evaporate. Then both partners, feeling uncomfortable with the detachment and distance, would resolve their differences and commence their destructive cycle again.

Many people avoid intimacy because of concern that if they allow themselves to be vulnerable they **might** get hurt. The reality is that if you choose to be vulnerable and intimate, it is not a matter of whether you **might** be hurt. You **will** be hurt. Pain is an inevitable component of intimacy. It is not possible to feel absolutely safe within a relationship. Once you let another person into your world, you become vulnerable. You don't feel hurt by people with whom you are just marginally involved. You experience pain with those who are closest to you: when they are sick or angry, when you feel rejected or abandoned, or ultimately, when they die. The only alternative you have, if you want to avoid that hurt, is to isolate yourself and avoid intimacy.

---

### EXERCISE 11

In your notebook, draw an intimacy meter and number it from zero to 10. Now, place marks that represent the maximum and minimum amounts of intimacy that you would be comfortable with at this point in your relationship and a second set of marks that correspond to what you project your partner's maximum and minimum comfort level with intimacy would be.

Notice any discrepancy between the two sets of marks and project what that might mean for your relationship.

---

If you discover from this exercise that you and your spouse have widely discrepant capacities for intimacy, we encourage you to approach opportunities to increase closeness with caution. Many couples, prematurely encouraged by their initial progress after they read self-help books, or after a few weeks of marital counseling, become disappointed when the distance increases or the peace turns to fighting. Do not attempt to force, seduce, or cajole your partner into increased intimacy. Efforts to push the degree of intimacy beyond his or her comfort level will likely be met with resistance and protectiveness. What you are getting is the most that he or she can give to you *at the current level of trust.* We encourage you to approach increased intimacy with caution. Be aware when you are reaching your limit of vulnerability, and let your partner know if you feel scared. Look for signs that your partner may be extending beyond his or her zone of comfort.

# Pseudo-Intimacy

Unfortunately, some people confuse extreme dependency with their partner as the ultimate in being intimate. Dependency and intimacy are not necessarily related. In a relationship based upon dependency, the couple may appear close, but their connection is not based upon a foundation of trust. Rather, the dependent partner acts out of a fear of being abandoned by his mate. Consequently, he or she does not set any boundaries, does not openly share feelings and opinions, and has trouble distinguishing thoughts and feelings from the partner's. Virtually every action the dependent partner takes is in concert with the partner's wishes.

> *To momentarily merge with another in the experience we call intimacy, we must be able to emerge again. Otherwise it's not intimacy and closeness—it's fusion and dependency. We need a healthy sense of self so we can count on ourselves to take care of ourselves.* *

* Melody Beattie, *Beyond Co-Dependency,* San Francisco: Harper & Row, 1989.

True emotional intimacy requires a knowledge of your own wants and needs and the honesty to express them. If you consistently subjugate your needs, your wants, and your boundaries to your partner's, you compromise your honesty. And without honesty there can be no trust.

*Todd loved to ski and play baseball, but because Trudy did not like these sports, he gave them up for her. He stayed home because Trudy felt his participation in sports interfered with their being close. He complied but was resentful. Trudy, on the other hand, gave up her book club and yoga, because she, too, felt that this is what an intimate couple would do. As their relationship progressed, so did their resentment. Both had given up their self-development and self-nurturing, and each was feeling empty.*

The dangers of dependency are perhaps most clearly illustrated when both partners in a relationship fall into this category. In this type of marriage, each mate carefully looks out for the other's needs. This type of mutually dependent marriage has often been acclaimed as the ideal marriage: two people, each anticipating the other's needs, and fulfilling every wish. This sounds pretty good, but unfortunately, the ideal is much better than the reality.

*John and Lisa want to go to dinner. Lisa would like to go out to an Italian restaurant, but knowing John likes Chinese food suggests, "Why don't we go to that little Chinese place?" John, who is really in a mood for a steak, but wanting to please Lisa, replies, "Okay, that sounds fine."* **Neither ends up getting what he or she wants.**

That is the irony of the mutually dependent relationship. Both wish to please, but neither is satisfied. Dependent partners are often very polite, pleasant people and, in a sense, act **too** nice to each other. Rarely do they directly express their anger, rather they bury it until it festers into resentment. They literally kill the relationship with kindness. In addition, because neither is really honest about their wants and needs, a feeling of distrust builds in the relationship.

To be truly intimate, both partners need to be completely honest with each other. Otherwise there can be only limited trust, and vulnerability becomes a risk. This includes the sharing of wants, needs, and the whole spectrum of feelings. In a truly honest and intimate marriage both partners clearly state their needs. If we were to view this type of couple making the decision about where to eat it would appear like this:

Joe wants to go to an Italian restaurant, and states,

"I'd like to go to that little Italian place for dinner."

Joan, who just had Italian food for lunch states,

"I'm not much in the mood for Italian food. That's what I ate for lunch. I'm in the mood for a steak."

They disagree, but at least each is clear about what the other wants, and they are prepared to negotiate cleanly. This type of relationship sounds selfish to many people, but the net result is clarity and honesty. No distrust builds. Whether they like what their partner says or not, each is usually clear about where their partner stands.

If your goal truly is to increase the trust and intimacy in your relationship, the surest way to get there is through open and honest communication. If you find it difficult to say no in your relationship and to set boundaries, it will be difficult to achieve true emotional intimacy.

## EXERCISE 12

Over the next twenty-four hours, pick three instances to set your limits and say *no* to your partner. When you do, pay attention to your reaction and to your partner's. Write down your observations in your notebook.

## DAY 13

# *Understanding Marital*
# *Communication*

Ask any person with marital problems what the primary
difficulty is with their relationship and, almost inevitably, that person will tell you "We don't communicate."
Yet in all the years we've spent working with couples in
marital counseling, we have yet to encounter a couple
who did not communicate. The problem isn't a lack of
communication. The problem is that **couples communicate more than they realize!**

### *The Myth of Noncommunication*

If you caringly stroke your partner's arm you communicate a message. If you rant and rave at your spouse,
that, too, communicates a message. Even if you walk
out of the room without saying a single word, communication has taken place. You and your spouse have been
communicating. **There is no such thing as not communicating.** Everything you say and do communicates a
message. The problem in marriage is not a matter of

simply communicating, it is a matter of communicating effectively.

Communication is a three-step process: **For communication to take place, one person must send a message, and another person must receive it and then interpret it.** Consequently, for truly effective communication to take place, the person sending the message must do an effective job sharing it and the person receiving the message must do an effective job at both listening and then interpreting. With both people viewing every interaction through their own personal kaleidoscope, there is much room for distortion.

As the following example demonstrates, what might seem to be even the simplest of communications is open to a great deal of personal distortion:

*Tim and Barbara entered marital counseling having made a mutual decision to get a divorce. One single incident had occurred a week prior that had crystallized this decision in their minds. Tim related the events of that night:*

TIM: *I couldn't sleep, I was tossing and turning, and I didn't want to wake Barbara, so I went downstairs to watch TV. I thought it would put me to sleep.*
BARBARA: *I woke up and he wasn't in bed. I was concerned, so I went downstairs to see what the problem was.*
TIM: *She came down and was obviously angry. I could tell by her face and by her body language. She just looked angry.*
BARBARA: *I was not. I wasn't the least bit angry. I was just concerned and scared.*

*As the story unfolded, Tim became angry because he believed that Barbara was unjustifiably angry with him.*

*His anger spilled over to early that morning. When he didn't give her the usual kiss after his shower, she asked: "So don't I get a good-morning kiss?"*

*Tim, now fuming, replied: "Why should I, you were a real bitch last night, why set myself up?"*

From that point the argument escalated until both agreed that their relationship was ready for the scrap heap. Because Tim had interpreted Barbara's body language without clarifying it with Barbara, he became trapped in his misinterpretation and the events snowballed into a near catastrophe.

### Interpreting Ambiguous Information

Not all communications get so easily distorted. Certainly you have many conversations with your spouse every day in which there seem to be no communication problem. Why are some conversations so prone to distortion? One possible answer can be found in the following simple figure. If you and most any other person looked at it, both of you would be likely to describe it similarly.

It's a circle. Not much to interpret. It is a simple, unambiguous image without a lot of personal meaning. However, that is where the problem comes in. Few things in life are as uncomplicated as a circle. The more ambiguity or complexity there is in the situation, the more room there is for variation in interpretations.

---

### EXERCISE 13

Look at the pictures that follow and write down in your notebook what you think just happened in each of the pictures, and what you believe each person is feeling. Then, go to two other people and ask them to interpret what they think has happened and what they believe each of the people in the pictures is feeling.

---

You can see from this exercise that we all interpret situations somewhat differently. Because the first picture contains little information and is unclear, the number of interpretations are nearly endless, and each person can project more of their own personal experiences into the picture. The second picture is open to interpretation, too, but because it contains more detail, the number of interpretations are limited. The point is that as any object or issue becomes more ambiguous, the possibility of personal interpretation grows at an incredibly fast rate.

# Learning How to Communicate

Communication is your way of sharing with your partner how you experience a situation, as it likewise is an opportunity for your partner to share his or her experience. Without that sharing, each of you is left to interpret your partner's experience. The only information you possess has been filtered through your own perception. Without effective communication you never learn to understand accurately how any given situation looks to your partner through his personal kaleidoscope. The goal of effective communication is to allow you to understand your partner's perception as clearly and unambiguously as possible and to give your partner the same opportunity to understand your own perception.

The next few chapters separate effective communication into two components: **effective sharing** and **effective listening.** These are not distinct issues, however, they are inseparably intertwined. If you share effectively, your partner will be encouraged to listen without feeling a need to act defensively, and if you listen effectively, it will be easier for your partner to share.

You already know how to communicate; you've known that since your infancy. You learned the power of verbal communication when you first cried, signaling that you were in some way uncomfortable. You also learned the magic of touch as a mode of communication. Sometimes the tactile message was soothing, at other times it was distressing, but you learned that every touch carried a definite meaning. Even the absence of being touched carried a strong message. As you grew, so did the number of communication tools you learned. You learned the effectiveness of the spoken word, and later, the written word. You learned how a tone of voice could enhance or emphasize a message. You learned the powerful impact of a simple glance, and you learned to interpret facial expressions and hand gestures, all skills that have now long been taken for granted. You even learned the commanding message conveyed by absolute silence.

All of your patterns and skills of communicating have been learned. Without ever consciously practicing or honing the tools, and most likely without ever once attending a class to develop your communication skills, you have shaped a style of sending and receiving messages for yourself. The tools you use to communicate with the world are no doubt the most effective ones you know. However, they are not the only tools available, nor the most effective ones.

### Effective Communication

Days 15–17, and later, day 22 contain a number of rules for effective communication. These rules offer no magical solutions. Simply reading and understanding them will not alter your communication pattern. Before you even look at the rules, it is essential that you appreciate to what extent communication is actually a matter of subjective interpretation. Then, by implementing **all** the rules on a **consistent** basis, you will be able to minimize any distortions.

At first glance, these rules may appear to be simple, even simplistic; however, to implement them will require a great deal of effort and concentration. When you initially use them, you are likely to feel awkward, possibly even silly, but it is essential that you take the time to learn and practice them until they become almost routine. Once they are added to your communications toolbox they will significantly enhance your relationship skills.

Obviously, it would be ideal if both you and your partner used these rules consistently. But since this book is focused on *your* ability to bring change to the process of marital communication, do not distract yourself by judging your partner's level of miscommunication. If you alone follow the rules, you can lessen the amount of distortion that ordinarily takes place in your communications and de-escalate the destructiveness of your disagreements. **Remember, you are and have been communicating.** Your new challenge is to maximize the effectiveness of that communication.

## EXERCISE 14

In your notebook make a list of three things you resent about your partner, three things you appreciate about him or her, and three actions you regret having taken since your relationship began.

Next to the nine entries, indicate which of these sentiments have been communicated to your partner verbally, which have been communicated nonverbally, and which have not been communicated at all.

List your reasons for not communicating all the sentiments directly and assess whether you wish to communicate clearly those sentiments that have not previously been shared.

## DAY 15

# *Effective Sharing*

Some people make the mistake of thinking that the more they talk, the more effective they will be at communicating. However, you can talk forever and still not communicate effectively. Indeed, sometimes talking too much can actually impede the process of effective sharing. Effective communication has little to do with the quantity of the sharing. Rather, the keys to effective sharing are in the quality of what is shared and in the clarity with which it is communicated. To share effectively, you must fulfill three requirements:

1. You must share in a way that encourages the other person to listen to you.
2. You must clearly express what you intend to say, so that there is no room for misinterpretation on the listener's part.
3. Your nonverbal cues, such as facial expression, tone of voice, and body language, must be consistent with what you say.

## *Encouraging Your Partner to Listen*

Having a partner who doesn't listen, or who incorrectly reads things into what is said, is aggravating and frustrating. Frequently, the situation feels hopeless. You cannot force him/her to pay attention to what you say nor can you coerce him/her into listening with an open mind.

However, because your partner is a free agent who thinks and acts on his/her own, this does not mean that you lack influence upon your partner's willingness to listen. There are a number of changes that you can initiate in your communication pattern that will encourage your partner to attend to what you are saying. The following rules are intended for just that purpose: to help you make changes that may invite your partner to listen more attentively.

RULE 1: *If your partner appears absorbed in something else at a time when you want to talk, request that he/she listen to you or have him/her suggest an alternative time.*

Obviously, if you want to make sure that your partner is going to listen, you need to make sure he/she is available. If your mate is totally absorbed in something, he/she is less likely to be receptive to what you have to say. Consequently, in order to assure that what you have to say gets adequate attention, simply tell your spouse you need to talk, and ask for his/her full attention. If your partner indicates either verbally or by a lack of undivided attention, that he/she is absorbed in something (even though it may seem trivial to you), explain that you have something to share and get a commitment as to when he/she will be available to listen. If you feel that what you have to say cannot be delayed, indicate the urgency of the situation, but be aware that your partner may be somewhat less accessible than you might like.

> RULE 2: *When sharing concerns or feelings with your partner, begin your statements with "I," or preferably "I feel (sad, angry, etc.)."*

This is called *"I"-language.* If you begin a sentence with the word *you,* there is a strong probability that your partner may interpret what you are saying to be threatening or accusatory. Rather than attending to what you are trying to say, your spouse will likely be plotting a defensive reply before all the words are out of your mouth.

Example: *You don't touch me as much as you used to. You just don't seem to be affectionate anymore.*

His/her typical response to such a statement will be a defensive one, possibly followed by a comment that puts you back on the defensive.

Example: *That's because I am so tired at night. If you worked as hard as I did, you'd find out why I don't have any energy left at the end of the day.*

Frequently this type of interaction escalates into a series of mutual accusations rather than a clear discussion of the issue. One note of caution: Beginning your sentences with *"I* think that *you . . ."* or *"I* feel that *you . . ."* has the same effect as beginning your sentences with the word *you.* In both of these situations, even though the sentence begins with *"I,"* the responsibility is laid on the shoulders of the other person.

Using the term *we* is similarly ineffective. Think about the difference in impact that each of the following sentences would have if you heard them from your spouse:

> *I love you.*
> *We love each other.*

The first is a personal and intimate statement, while the second not only lacks intimacy but makes an assumption about what the other person is feeling. This habit is one very quick way of unintentionally provoking a fight. You can't read your partner's mind. If you say *"We love each other,"* or *"We need to talk,"* you are making an assumption about the way your spouse feels.

Instead of beginning your sentences with *you* or *we,* talk about what you **want** and what you **feel.** If you make a statement like: *"I feel lonely. I would like it if you would touch me more often,"* your partner has no need to be defensive. You are not saying that he/she is doing anything wrong. You are simply saying that you have a need for more touching. Maybe that need is connected with the way you were raised as a child, or maybe it has to do with some other events in your life, but nowhere in your statement is there an accusation that your partner is at fault. If your spouse does get defensive, be supportive. Let him/her know that you did not mean your statement as an accusation, but merely as a statement of your need.

Many individuals we talk to in counseling at first are concerned that talking about "I" is being selfish. They were raised to think always of the other person. Remember, however, that the ability to state your personal wants and needs is a key to being able to share effectively.

Even consistent use of "I"-language does not guarantee that your partner will understand what your needs are. In fact, many people can more clearly articulate what they *don't* want rather than what they *do* want.

RULE 3: *Be clear in stating what you want, rather than expressing what you don't want.*

It is fine if you state what you do *not* want, but always follow that with a statement that defines what you desire instead. For example, had we stated rules 1 and 2 in terms of what you *shouldn't* do, they would read like this:

*Don't talk to your partner if he/she seems absorbed in something else.*

*Don't begin your sentences with "you" or "we."*

You would probably look at the two rules and feel very frustrated and constrained. You have no idea what you can do as an alternative. However, by explaining "I"-language, you now have a clear alternative. The rules do not seem as limiting or intimidating. This is what happens in relationships. If you continually tell your partner what you *don't* want, but are not clear about what you *do* want, your partner will eventually become very frustrated and angry. As we mentioned previously, stating what you want is an important tool in setting your boundaries.

RULE 4: *Rather than asking questions, rephrase them as statements that reflect your feelings.*

Many times questions are used not as a way of eliciting information, but as a way of trapping someone. For instance, you might say to your partner: *"Why didn't you let the dog out today?"* This is a setup. In truth, you really don't care *why* he/she didn't let the dog out. You are expressing your displeasure, not asking for a clarification. No matter what the reply is, you are going to express your anger.

Instead of asking a question, rephrase it to an "I feel/ I want" statement, such as, *"I really get upset when the dog is left inside. I end up cleaning up after him, and then I end up feeling angry with you. Please let him out from now on."* In this example, avoiding the use of a question and substituting an "I" statement, eliminates the need for your partner to reply in a defensive manner. All he/she has to do is listen effectively.

Effective sharing is not necessarily friendly communication or happy talk, nor does it always initially feel constructive. Sometimes it involves pain for you and for your partner. At other times it can involve tremendous closeness. Always, it involves hard work. What effective sharing does is leave the door open so that issues can be resolved. Through effective sharing you can give your partner a glimpse into your world as perceived through your frame of reference. There is no other way your mate can understand what your perspective looks like. Without your input, everything your partner sees carries his/her unique color of distortion. Effective sharing allows you and your partner to hear each other's issues clearly, and it encourages both to listen effectively. And, when the difficult issues are resolved, it is likely to promote a feeling of intimacy.

---

### EXERCISE 15

Write down one statement that clearly reflects an aspect of your partner's behavior that you would like him or her to change. Remember to start with *"I."*

Example: *I would like you to stop coming home so late.*

Now expand on that statement by writing a list of exactly what you would like instead of that behavior. Be very specific and concrete. It is **not** sufficient to write a statement like: *I would like you to come home*
*Continued*

*on time from now on.* That is not specific enough. Write down in detail, exactly what you want.

Example: *I would like you home by 6:00 a couple of times each week. If you intend to work late, I would like to know the night before, so that I can make plans for myself. If something comes up at the last minute that changes your plans, I would like to be called as soon as possible.*

Below that, write a list of any feelings you have about the behavior you would like to see your partner change. (See appendix A for a list of feeling words).

Example: *I feel angry, frustrated, and jealous.*

Now put the feelings together with the "wants" and integrate them into a complete statement. Keep it brief, no more than eight sentences. Practice saying it a couple of times just so you get a sense of how it feels to verbalize an "I feel/I want" statement.

Example: *I feel angry, frustrated, and unimportant when you come home late for dinner. I also sometimes get jealous, even though my mind knows that you are really at work. I would like you to come home by 6:00 a couple of times a week so I can spend more time with you. If you know the night before that you will be late, let me know, but if you are unavoidably detained by work, call me, so that I don't end up feeling discounted.*

You may choose whether or not to share this statement with your partner. However, if you do, remember to pick a time when your partner is not absorbed in something, or ask him/her to suggest an alternative time.

# Verbal Clarity and Consistency

Sharing is only half of a two-step process. No matter how effectively one partner shares, the overall process of communication can be crippled if the other partner does not listen effectively. You cannot make your partner listen, but what you can do is provide an atmosphere that will make it easier for him/her to hear what you express. One way that is certain to turn off your partner is to bring up arguments that put him/her on the defensive.

RULE 5: *Avoid the use of statements that tend to drag up the past. One way of limiting these kinds of statements is to avoid the use of* absolutes—*words such as* always, never, whenever, every time.

If you use an *absolute,* invariably the other person will cite any exceptions that have occurred. You will end up arguing about what happened previously instead of what is occurring right now. The following example is from Bill Cosby's *Love and Marriage:*

"I think you should know I am really tired of your always saying that I'm an urban village idiot."

"No, dear," you reply, "you're not paying attention. I don't *always* say that you're an urban idiot. I have only said it *twice:* last Tuesday evening at your mother's and last May seventeenth at church. Our relationship would be better if you kept score."

"And you always *correct me like that.*"

"No, again, not always: *just a few thousand times when you're wrong.*"

"But I'm not wrong. I remember *precisely* what you've said to me."

When you use an absolute, your point gets buried in a debate about the past and your present needs get lost. Instead of using an absolute, begin a statement with "I" and speak in terms of the present. For example, instead of making a statement like *"You never initiate sex anymore,"* change it to: "I would like you to be more assertive in initiating sex."

A second way of avoiding dragging up the past is not to bring up topics that are more than twenty-four-hours old. When arguing, many people will bring up past events as "ammunition" to prove their point. Frequently, these types of statements have a way of backfiring because they deflect the discussion from the present and drag both parties back into a debate about what happened days, weeks, or even months ago. Example:

PARTNER 1: *This is the third time this week you didn't call.*

PARTNER 2: *That's not true, I called every day except Tuesday.*

PARTNER 1: *No! If you remember, on Monday . . .*

If you want your partner to listen to you, make your point in a way that is relevant to the present. No one can change the past. Besides, each of us views the past through our unique frame of reference. If one person tries to prevail by using prior events as examples, the discussion frequently deteriorates into a debate about who is right in their perception of the past issues. This is completely irrelevant to the point that is being made about the present. Instead, stick with the present, begin your sentence with "I", and state what you want and/or what you feel. Example:

PARTNER 1: *I would like you to call me as soon as you know that you are going to be delayed. This way, I can put dinner off for a little while, or the rest of the family can eat before you get home.*

Occasionally it is necessary for people to discuss past events. If you feel the need to do so, first check out your motivation. Assuming your intent is not to demean or disprove your partner, then go ahead. When you do, invoke all of the rules of effective communication.

The previous five rules are basic to all personal communication and can be effective tools in all of your relationships with friends and family. However, be aware that these rules only work effectively when the ultimate goal is to be somewhat more intimate. Frequently, these same rules are not effective in a work environment, where one person has power over another. Vulnerability can often be detrimental in that type of hierarchical atmosphere. Be cautious how you incorporate these skills into your workplace.

Because your body language, facial expressions, and tone of voice speak as loudly and as clearly as the words you utter, it is not uncommon for these actions to send messages that are incompatible with your words. Although you may believe that you communicate with words, it often is nonverbal communication that more accurately reflects your true feelings. Rolling your eyes, folding your arms, using a patronizing tone of voice, or other such nonverbal language may strongly color the meaning of whatever words are spoken. These actions convey secondary messages, or *meta-messages,* which are underlying messages covertly communicated. For example, if you say to your partner, *"Let me help you hang that picture,"* the overt message seems clear enough. You want to help your partner hang a picture. But there may be any number of possible meta-messages that get communicated without ever saying them in words.

One possibility might be: *"You seem to be struggling, and I just want to help."* Or another might be: *"I don't think you do a very good job at hanging pictures. I am more competent than you."* A third might be: *"I get afraid when I see you acting so independently."*

Meta-messages are no less important than overt messages. They get interpreted along with the spoken words, and in many instances can actually hold more weight than the words themselves. Sometimes these covert messages are shared and received clearly without either partner being consciously aware that a message has been communicated.

Remember, your partner will interpret your communications based upon what you say, how you say it, and what your underlying meta-message conveys. All this is then processed through his or her unique frame of reference. Therefore, the more vague or inconsistent your nonverbal messages are, the more room there is for misinterpretation.

RULE 6: *Be consistent in both your words and your actions. If you or your partner notice inconsistencies, assess whether the multiple messages represent conflicting feelings within you.*

If you smile at your spouse while saying you're angry, it may be difficult for your partner to believe that you are really upset. Two conflicting messages have been sent, and the inconsistencies between them can play havoc with the process of effective communication.

*Ron was able to express his anger toward Cheryl, but whenever he did, he would smile and use a very indifferent tone. His words said clearly that he was angry, but his facial expression and tone of voice conveyed a sense of acceptance or conciliation. Because this diffused the impact of his words, Cheryl would often dismiss the importance of Ron's anger and continue her actions. This in turn left Ron frustrated and led him to accumulate a reservoir of unresolved feelings. Occasionally, when the reservoir would overfill, Ron's dam would burst, and Cheryl would be inundated with a flood of his feelings, which on the surface appeared to be inappropriate to the situation.*

---

### EXERCISE 16

Tune into a soap opera or situation comedy on television, and watch it for about fifteen minutes. Pay attention to how many times the characters break the rules discussed in this chapter and the previous one. Also, notice what the reaction of the other characters are when the rules do get broken.

*Continued*

Now turn off the sound. See how much you can understand about emotions or attitude from just watching people without hearing any words. After a few minutes, turn the volume back on, but turn your back to the television, and notice how much tone of voice conveys.

Which do you feel is most important in conveying the meaning of a conversation: actions? tone of voice? spoken words?

During the next twenty-four hours, be aware of conversations with family members, friends, and workmates. Notice what your reaction is any time one of the rules gets broken. Also, be aware of how your body language and voice influence people around you. At the same time notice how you are influenced by the actions and voice inflections of others.

When you feel that you have absorbed the basic concepts provided in this chapter and the previous (Day 15 and 16), continue on. Do not worry about your partner and his/her skills. You cannot change your partner's behavior, only your own. Use the information in this chapter to improve your own skills. Because your relationship is part of a dynamic process, any changes that you make in your behavior will ultimately alter your marriage.

# *Effective Listening*

Hearing, listening, and **effective listening** are three completely different processes. Hearing involves collecting sound waves with your ears and processing them in your brain. Since you began reading this page, your ears have absorbed many background noises. However, with your attention riveted to this book, few if any of those sounds were noticed. Your ears heard the noises, but you did not listen to them. Take a second to listen to those background noises before resuming your reading.

Listening involves both hearing and paying attention. If you are watching television and your spouse is speaking to you at the same time, your ears absorb sound waves from both sources, but your mind can concentrate on only one. If you become annoyed with the interruption, you may become so distracted that you don't listen to either one.

**Effective listening** is a process designed to clarify and confirm messages from your partner and involves a great deal more than simply attending to the words your ears collect. It is a learned technique that incorporates not only hearing and listening, but involves careful observation, interpretation of your partner's actions, and verification of the accuracy of those interpretations.

Effective listening is critically important in the process of marital communication. It is your only window into your spouse's world. Since your reality is colored by your frame of reference, there is no way you can truly know what your mate is experiencing without a personal description from him/her. If your partner doesn't feel comfortable enough to share these perceptions, or you do not listen when they are shared, a valuable opportunity for understanding is lost. Effective listening is an opportunity for you to convey to your mate an attitude that even though your perceptions and values may differ, his/her experiences are important to you.

Understanding the rules in this chapter will not immediately transform you into an effective listener. It's not that easy. It will take a conscientious effort for you to implement the rules on a consistent basis. You are used to another way of thinking and doing things. Old, familiar habits are hard to break. Simply opening your ears and shutting your mouth won't transform you into an effective listener. Effective listening involves stifling your instinct to defend yourself, remaining nonjudgmental, accepting your partner as an equal, and confirming that his/her opinions and beliefs have value.

Even after you learn to implement the skills outlined in this chapter, some lapses will occasionally occur. Each of us sometimes allows our concentration to drift while attending to a conversation, especially when we are tired, disinterested, upset, or preoccupied with other thoughts. However, by adhering to the rules that follow, you can minimize your distractibility and maximize your understanding in conversations with your partner.

RULE 7: *Let your partner know that you are listening attentively. If you are not fully ready to attend to what your partner is saying, give him/her an alternative time when you will be totally available.*

Continuing to watch TV or reading a newspaper while your partner talks does not give him/her a feeling that you are listening attentively. Likewise, if you yawn, check your watch, walk into another room, or in any other way appear disinterested, your mate will have little incentive for opening up. One excellent way of letting your partner know you are listening is to make eye contact. If you are looking at your spouse, and appear to be attentive to what he/she is saying, this will encourage further communication.

In addition, verbally acknowledge what your partner is communicating by simply stating, *"I understand what you are saying, tell me more,"* or some similar phrase that asserts you are being attentive. A well-placed word now and then confirms that you are emotionally present.

Sometimes your partner will need to talk at a time that is not opportune for listening: it's the middle of your favorite TV show or a critical point in a football game. Maybe you are too angry to attend to what your mate is saying, or just tired and need to nap. Whatever the reason, sometimes you are just not ready to listen. If this is the case, be honest about your unavailability and give your partner a reasonable alternative when you will be able to listen. **Be specific** about the time.

Example: *I would prefer not to talk right now, because I am very tired. Let me take a nap for about an hour, then I can give you my full attention.*

Obviously, if your partner is in the middle of a crisis, this will not work effectively. He/she will require your immediate attention. For most marital issues, however, a short delay is usually acceptable. What will not be acceptable for most mates is if you either pretend to listen but absorb very little or if you shut your partner out completely and communicate that he/she is bothering you.

If you have an issue that keeps you from listening, be open in sharing it with your mate. Share your feeling and, set an alternative time to talk.

Example: *I feel so angry that I don't feel I can discuss the issue right now, I need to take a walk. Maybe when I get back I will be able to discuss it.*

RULE 8: *Clarify what you have heard.*

In any conversation, and particularly during a disagreement, let your spouse know that you are listening attentively by clarifying what you have heard. This accomplishes two things. First, it communicates to your partner that you are listening and are interested in clearly understanding what is being said. Second, if there has been some sort of misunderstanding, it provides your mate with an opportunity to restate his/her remarks.

The best way to clarify is to summarize briefly, in your own words, what you believe your partner is saying. For example, if you were to clarify what has been said so far in this chapter, you would say: *"What I understand you to be saying is that listening effectively is extremely important in a conversation, but sometimes we are distracted. One basic rule for listening effectively is to make eye contact or in some way let your partner know you are listening. The second is . . ."*

If I felt you understood what I said, I would confirm that you were correct. If, on the other hand, I felt misunderstood or that you missed an important point, I would share with you that some information was missed or misunderstood, and I would attempt to clear up the confusion by restating what I was attempting to convey.

It is extremely important that you do not make any

assumptions about what your spouse is communicating. Many times, especially when a couple is experiencing conflict, each partner acts as if the other is an enemy, rather than assuming that he/she is a teammate wishing to heal the relationship. If you find yourself making any assumptions based either upon verbal or nonverbal cues from your spouse, clarify them using the same technique as above.

Example: *I feel that you have been angry at me since you walked in the door. I just wanted to check that out with you so I can understand what is going on.*

RULE 9: *Listen without interrupting.*

Of the rules for effective listening, this is possibly the most difficult to implement. Under some circumstances, it can be extremely difficult to listen to your spouse without interrupting to defend yourself. However, simply by listening attentively, you can demonstrate to your mate that you want to know what is on his/her mind. Interrupting before your partner has a chance to complete a thought indicates a lack of respect. If you truly do not understand what your mate is saying, then ask for clarification. However, be careful not to ask a "setup" question designed to put your partner on the defensive. In addition, clarify to make certain your understanding is accurate.

Days 15–17 were designed to help you gain understanding of how the world looks from your spouse's perspective and to help you share your frame of reference with your mate. This in turn can add depth and intimacy to the relationship. Throughout the remainder of this book, and it is hoped throughout the remainder of your life, the groundwork will help you establish a fuller repertoire of skills. Follow the rules conscientiously, and more important, understand and embrace the concepts behind them. As with athletic abilities, if you cease to use your communication skills on a regular basis, you will become inconsistent at implementing them.

---

### EXERCISE 17

Do this exercise preferably, with your spouse, but if you don't yet trust your skills of being able to listen effectively to your mate, choose another person you trust and with whom you feel comfortable.

When you feel ready, approach that person (don't do it over the phone) and say, "I would like you to share one thing you would like me to change about myself." As you approach, notice what your body is feeling. Notice particularly any tension.

While this person is sharing, utilize the listening rules. Do not interrupt, do not get defensive, and do not argue. Do not respond in any way, even if your intent is constructive. Just listen.

1. You may ask for clarification, if you do not understand precisely what the person is trying to communicate, or;
2. When you believe you have a clear understanding of what is being said, acknowledge it by repeating back what you have heard.

Do not interpret what you thought was meant. Just repeat what was said nonjudgmentally. Be especially careful not to degrade what is being shared by responding in a condescending tone or with a disgusted look on your face. **Remember, it is not necessary that you agree, nor is there any requirement that you make the changes that are being asked for.** In addi-
*Continued*

tion, keep in mind that the person who is sharing with you is doing you a favor. He/she is giving you some valuable feedback.

After you complete the assignment make an honest appraisal of your own feelings and behavior during the exercise, and jot down some notes. Particularly notice if you felt like interrupting, defending yourself, walking out of the room, or violating any of the rules in this chapter. This may give you an indication of ways in which you sometimes interfere with the process of open communication in your marital relationship. Also be aware of the contributions you made toward keeping the discussion in line. Based upon your experience during this assignment, note any alterations you would like to make in your own listening behavior.

# Sexual Communication

Sex holds an especially high place of importance in our society. We see it plastered all over TV, on billboards, in every form of visual media. We hear sexual innuendo on the radio and in casual conversation. Sex sells books and newspapers, lures us into movies, and helps peddle every product from cigarettes to underwear. Our children are exposed to it, and we as adults are continuously inundated with it. However, these daily doses are the exaggerations and distortions about sex, designed to grab our attention. Very little of what we see and hear prepares us for the realities of a sexual relationship. Much of this informal sex education distorts our expectations about sex and sexual relationships.

Sex is not a simple skill like eating with a knife and fork. It is an issue of great complexity. It is affected by your general physical health, hormone levels, mood, environment, cultural and historical background, religious beliefs, general psychological state, age, medications or other chemical substances, learned skills, as well as many other issues. Although your relationship with your mate is usually the major component of your total sexual relationship, it is only one segment of the whole. Damage to any one of the pieces can lead to sexual difficulties.

In a sense, sex is merely another form of communication, and as such, our previous caveat—*There is no such thing as not communicating*—applies to sex equally well. You do communicate about sex, whether you realize it or not. The way you dress, the way you move, what you say, and how you say it, all convey sexual messages. Turn on any soap opera and look and listen to the characters, and you will see how much information they share about sex and their sexuality without any overt discussion. There is no way to avoid communicating about sex and, as with any form of communication, the more ambiguous you are about your sexual needs or your sexual feelings, the more your partner will have to interpret and misinterpret.

You are an expert on sex. You know more about your personal sexual needs and desires than any person alive. Likewise, your partner is an expert on his or her own body. By honestly sharing your wants and needs, and by listening to your partner's, you can remove a lot of guesswork and tension from your sexual relationship. That is why your communication skills are so important in the area of sexuality.

Sharing your feelings or your needs before or during a sexual encounter is an important part of the communication process. Your needs and your partner's change from one sexual encounter to the other. They even change from moment to moment within a single sexual experience. Consequently, the only way you can be in touch with each other's desires is with constant communication. Mind reading doesn't work. Your partner can't know all your wants and needs unless you share them.

*Share your sexual needs and wants in a way that encourages your partner to listen.* Do not expect your partner to read your mind. The most common mistake people tend to make in the sexual arena is that they tend to complain about what they *don't* enjoy about the sexual experience rather than asking for what they do enjoy. If you continue to complain, your partner is likely to become frustrated, angry, and turned off. When you share what you want, follow the rules of effective communication presented in the preceding chapters. This will encourage a process of mutual education.

Example: *I would like you to touch harder* (rather than: *You're tickling me*).

Example: *I would like you to initiate sex more frequently* (rather than: *I am getting tired of always having to initiate sex*).

A great deal of this book has been spent emphasizing the importance of boundaries, and in no place is that more important than in the area of sexuality. It is essential that both you and your partner feel free to set your sexual limits in a way that assures your safety and security. True sexual freedom includes the freedom to say no. In the long run, both partners suffer if either engages in a sexual act that feels painful, uncomfortable, or coerced. If you engage in any behavior that you find distasteful, even if it is simply an activity like eating a food you dislike, the tendency is to want to do it less frequently. For that reason, sexual partners who repeatedly engage in sexual acts out of a feeling of obligation or coercion usually find their sexual interest dwindling.

Some partners are afraid to set sexual limits, because they fear that it would hurt their partner's feelings. Tact is wonderful in sharing sexual concerns, but it should never inhibit your honesty. You cannot completely disguise sexual concerns. On one level or another your reservations, fears, or dislikes will get communicated. Even if you have not verbalized your concerns in the past, on some level your partner knows about your dissatisfaction. By honestly sharing those concerns, you bring the issue into the open, and eventually that leads to a stronger bond. If you are not open in sharing these feelings, not only will your sexual relationship suffer, but the trust in your relationship will be damaged. That can seriously undermine every other aspect of your marriage.

If you find a sexual act objectionable or if you are not in the mood for a sexual encounter, state that. However, be clear that you are rejecting the invitation and not your partner. The best way to do this is to assure your partner of your loving feelings toward him or her, but to reject the physical act. If possible, provide your partner with an alternative.

Example: *I am really not in the mood right now. I love you, but I would like to wait until a time when I'm not so tired. Tomorrow hopefully will be a better day. Maybe if we're both in a sexual frame of mind tomorrow morning we can try then.*

As we have said repeatedly in this book, the more you focus your attention on influencing your partner's behavior, the more powerless you feel. The exact same theme applies to sex. Your focus for sexual excitement should not be directed toward figuring out how to excite your partner sexually, but rather toward turning yourself on. Think about it: If your partner is not in a sexual mood, or if you incorrectly guess what your partner desires sexually, you can work forever, and he or she will never be turned on. On the other hand, if each of you is clear about communicating your sexual needs, neither of you has to guess what the other is wanting.

When the focus of sex becomes directed almost exclusively toward *turning on* your partner, or toward trying to read your partner's mind as to what he or she desires, sex becomes work, and the potential for sexual dysfunction is greatly increased. Erection and orgasm are reflexes that occur when your body reaches a certain level of excitement. If you are *working* on your spouse and not concentrating on your own pleasure, you will not reach the necessary level of arousal to achieve orgasm or erection. Work is counterproductive to arousal.

When we refer to sex in this chapter, we are referring to much more than intercourse. Sexual activity for couples refers to a whole spectrum of activity that may also include sexual fantasy, touching, gazing at each other, stroking, kissing, foreplay, and an indeterminable number of other activities. Couples who get centered on the genital nature of sexual activity often become so performance oriented that they miss much of the sensuality and enjoyment connected with other forms of sex play.

As you age and your marriage evolves, you will undergo physical and emotional changes. However, nothing in the aging process need eliminate a healthy sex life from your repertoire. Couples can maintain an active and exciting sexual relationship throughout a long marriage and into the golden years.

Do not underestimate the potential of this book for improving your sexual relationship. It contains some powerful tools for improving the quality and quantity of sex in your relationship. Every chapter you have read has relevance to your sexuality. If you doubt that, pick any chapter at random and reread it with an eye toward better understanding of your sexuality. In addition, Recommended Reading at the end of this volume lists a few books we recommend for expanding your knowledge and understanding of sexuality and sexual dysfunctions.

The point of this exercise is to demonstrate how eliminating performance pressure can enhance a sexual experience. In addition, it is designed to get you to focus on your own sexual pleasure rather than your partner's and to encourage you to explore other areas and techniques unconnected with genital sex.

## EXERCISE 18

This exercise is meant to be done with your marital partner. If either one of you is not open to such an experience, an alternative assignment is provided in Appendix C.

Before participating in this exercise it is extremely important that both participants agree that this assignment will not evolve into genital play or intercourse for at least three hours after the exercise has been completed. Any attempts to push this exercise beyond its intended limits will not only reduce the effectiveness of the exercise, but may undermine the trust in the relationship.

Both partners are to undress and lie in bed or in another place where both are comfortable. The partner who is reading this book should then touch the other partner all over his or her body, with the exception of the breast and genital areas. The other partner should lie quietly, just receiving the attention. Be creative in your touching and be totally selfish. Touch as you would a fur rug—feel the texture, the temperature of the different areas, the contours, etc. Allow it to be a sensual experience. Do not touch to give your partner pleasure or to turn him/her on in any way.

After about ten to fifteen minutes, reverse roles. The partner who was touching now lies quietly, while the other touches for his/her own pleasure.

# Winning the Battle; Losing the War

Although most people abhor dissension, it is a necessary ingredient in all relationships. Disagreements are an opportunity for expressing individuality and independence, and more important, they are a means for each mate to learn about the wants and needs of the partner. As each of us sees a different view of the world through our unique kaleidoscope, we are convinced of the validity of our individual perceptions. It is neither desirable nor possible to eliminate dissimilarities. To the contrary, these differences need to be accepted and even cherished as an opportunity to glimpse inside your partner— a chance to gain a clearer understanding of his or her unique perceptions as well as afford you a greater understanding of yourself.

Unfortunately, for many couples, these learning opportunities are squandered and lead to friction and pain rather than insight or empathy. Differences and disagreements become something to be feared and avoided rather than encouraged. This occurs, not necessarily because of any lack of desire, but usually because both of the combatants have attained varying levels of proficiency in the art of communication.

Your skill at settling disagreements is not innate. Like your ability to share and listen effectively, your proficiency at resolving differences and defending yourself is dependent upon survival skills acquired from various relationships throughout your life. You don't remember learning them, they just seemed to be there the first time you needed them. At some time earlier in your life, you found yourself in the middle of a verbal battle and you seized some familiar weapons to defend yourself. You didn't have time to evaluate which would work most effectively or which would have the fewest negative consequences. You simply latched on to whichever was most immediately available. Then, as you matured, you modified and honed those weapons into tools to fit the changing tides of your various relationships. Some of the skills you acquired were constructive, others destructive. Each relationship provided a new and unique challenger to your defenses and resulted in a new and refined set of skills.

When your spouse entered the picture, your unique style blended with your partner's to form a new pattern for dealing with disagreements. Differences may have been openly aired or not discussed at all. They may have involved loud and even violent confrontations or silent revenge. They may have taken the form of long-standing feuds or may have been quickly and consistently resolved by constructive discussions. Gradually, over the years, each of you learned to adapt to each other's style. Every time your mate's style changed, you fine-tuned your own. And for every refinement you made, your partner also adjusted, until your respective styles evolved into the characteristic pattern of fighting you use today.

By trial and error, by carefully observing the skills of others, or through reading books, some couples are able to achieve a constructive pattern of resolving disagreements. For these couples, disagreements become a tool for learning, change, and intimacy in their relationship. For many individuals, however, the reaction to conflict is reflexive, based upon a primitive need for survival. At the first hint of threat, a defensive umbrella is automatically deployed, with little evaluation of whether its use is constructive or destructive.

Scattered throughout the next few chapters you will find a number of quotes from a classic book called *The Art of War*, by Sun Tzu, a Chinese general and philosopher. The words were written more than 2,500 years ago as a treatise on the waging of war, but unfortunately they point to the many similarities that frequently exist in marital conflicts.

Although disagreement and even conflict is unavoidable in marriage, the ultimate aim of resolving dissension is to better the marriage. Unfortunately, this idealistic goal frequently gets buried in the emotional debris of the wars waged by many couples. Days 20–25 are devoted to describing some of the destructive methods couples use to deal with conflict in their relationship. They are designed to give you insight into your own characteristic pattern and that of your partner.

*"The true object of war is peace."*—Sun Tzu

In the following exercise, you will be building a kaleidoscope for your partner, similar to the one you did for yourself on Day 3.

### EXERCISE 19

Pick an issue on which you and your partner disagree, and look at it only from his or her viewpoint. Under each of the following categories, list at least one event or attribute that you feel may contribute to your mate's view on this issue. Here is a sample issue and examples of looking at it from a mate's viewpoint:

Issue: *He wants to buy a large car, and I want an economy-sized car.*

1. **Genetics**
   Example: *He is over six feet tall.*
2. **Environment**
   Example: *He does a lot of freeway driving.*
3. **Childhood Experiences**
   Example: *He was raised in an environment where status was important.*
4. **Traumas**
   Example: *He was in a serious traffic accident and may be somewhat nervous about smaller cars.*
5. **Adult Experiences**
   Example: *His friend John just got a new large car, and they are in a very competitive relationship.*

This exercise has nothing to do with whose viewpoint is right. Rather, it is to allow you to see that issues you and your partner disagree on can be a real opportunity to gain a greater understanding about how your partner perceives the world.

## DAY 20

# *Power Struggles*

Winning is wonderful. The only problem with winning in a marriage is that for one person to win, the other must lose. And if one of you loses, both of you end up paying a price. Unfortunately, many people view marital disagreements as an opportunity to test their skills at debating. Debate is a win/lose situation. Each debater tries to justify the righteousness of his/her opinion or the folly of the mate's. The marriage becomes a verbal tug-of-war. Ultimately this struggle between the two combatants spills over into other areas of the marriage. The battle cry becomes: *If you won't give in to me on verbal issues, I won't give in to you . . .*

1. in the bedroom
2. on financial matters
3. on being affectionate
4. on coming home from work when you want
5. on keeping the house clean
6. *(Fill in your own area of combat.)*

Ultimately, one partner ends up feeling dissatisfied and/or defeated and the relationship becomes scarred.

Think of any issue the two of you truly disagree on. What are the chances you could truly change your mate's point of view? Or that your partner might truly alter yours? Probably close to nil. One of you, more skilled in the art of debate, might grind the other down to the point of surrender, but ultimately it will be an empty victory. Unwilling submission raises resentment in the yielding partner and diminishes the respect that the victor has for him/her. Inevitably it will lead to increased distance and escalating conflict.

*"Soldiers in desperate straits lose the sense of fear. If there is no place of refuge, they will stand firm."*—Sun Tzu

With some couples, winning, or at least avoiding losing, becomes a way of life. Each is convinced that it is the other who is primarily responsible for any tension in the relationship. Consequently, one mate rigidly resolves to resist until the other shows some significant sign of changing. A stalemate develops as each waits patiently for the other to make the initial reforms. Rather than become allies, working toward a common goal, the two become combatants. Like warring factions with weapons drawn, each waits for the other to make the first move. Every movement and every word is scrutinized for some signal of danger. Paranoia plays an increasingly prominent role in the relationship. The trigger fingers get itchier, each trying to anticipate what treachery the other may be plotting. At the first anticipation of danger, one fires the verbal bullets, the other retaliates, and the battle rages until one combatant eventually capitulates.

*"In desperate situations you must fight."*—Sun Tzu

Sometimes the rules for this **power struggle** appear quite civilized; other times they are a no-holds-barred war. However, the object is always the same: Each time you fear that you are in a vulnerable position, you instinctively scramble out of that position, either by disengaging from the battle or by placing the other partner on the defensive. Power struggles are most frequent in relationships in which the partners avoid setting boundaries or set boundaries that are inflexible. Frequently these struggles represent a battle between one partner struggling for independence and a sense of freedom in the relationship, while the other partner feels threatened seeing the mate pulling away.

Inevitably in any power struggle one partner ends up the apparent winner and the other the apparent loser. Frequently, both feel as if they have lost. Rarely, if ever, do the two share victory. From this scenario, a never-ending sequence of one-upsmanship is encouraged.

As long as the two partners feel like adversaries, the battle will continue to rage; each feeling wounded and unloved and waiting for the other to change; neither taking a long look at his/her own behavior. Like two warring countries, each combatant points an accusing finger at the other. Each holds the other responsible for the war. Neither trusts the other enough to accept offerings of peace without a great deal of suspicion and apprehension. Cease-fires are not a time to celebrate, but rather become a time when every move by the opposition is scrutinized for some sign of sabotage. At the slightest sign—real or imagined—the war is renewed with increased intensity.

If you are in the middle of a power struggle you are at war. Each of you perceives the other as an enemy. Again, warring parties do not yield to pressure or even to caring advice from their enemies. Advice can never be accepted in good faith, but rather is viewed as suspiciously as a Trojan horse. Helping your partner understand and work through his/her problems is not the answer in a power struggle. Even good intentions may be misconstrued as an attack or as an attempt to be controlling.

*"Only one who knows the disastrous effects of a long war can realize the supreme importance of rapidity in bringing it to a close."*—Sun Tzu

## Cold Wars

Not all couples get into pitched battles. For some the struggle is silent, though just as divisive. There is no loud arguing, no verbal disagreement, and no overt differences. To friends on the outside, these quiet combatants often look like the perfect couple. However, these **cold wars** can be extremely venomous, and in some respects, can be even more dangerous for a relationship. At least when overt war is declared, both combatants are clear that there is trouble. In a cold war, one or both partners hold in their anger, subtly retaliating with obstructiveness and rebelliousness. Because there is no verbal acknowledgment of the problems, there is no dialogue; therefore no learning takes place and the tension continues to grow.

*Tom and Debbie had been married only a short time when he first took his secretary to lunch. Tom became aware that Debbie was jealous because of all the questions she was asking. She did not openly bring up the subject of infidelity, but nevertheless he avoided conflict in the marriage by keeping his relationship with his secretary strictly professional. A year later, Debbie became pregnant, the couple was feeling financially strapped, and each was quietly distancing himself from the other. Feeling resentful and estranged from Debbie, and wanting to talk with someone, Tom took his secretary for lunch, but this time he decided to keep it a secret from Debbie. When she inadvertently found out about the concealed lunch, Debbie's jealousy multiplied and her anger grew.*

*Debbie never raised her voice or expressed the fact that she was jealous and angry, but she began to check up on Tom. The more she checked up, the angrier Tom felt and the more secretive he became. Like two children getting even with each other, this couple continued to escalate their conflict. Two years later, after each had had an extramarital relationship and after a brief separation, the couple was able to enter counseling and confront each other with their issues.*

The following is an exercise for you and your spouse. It is designed to help the two of you reduce any power struggles that are occurring. Even though the exercise itself only takes ten minutes, make sure that both of you have twenty minutes available. That way you will not be rushed, and you will have a few minutes to digest the results after the exercise has been completed.

---

### EXERCISE 20

If your marital partner is not open to this experience, an alternative assignment is provided in appendix D.

Read the following instructions aloud: Find a comfortable spot away from the bedroom, turn the TV off, take the phone off the hook, and minimize any

*Continued*

potential distractions. Sit down facing each other, close enough to touch the other person.

To begin this exercise, the person who is now reading will be sharing feelings, and the other will be listening. The partner who is listening now chooses a soft object, such as a pillow, and hands it to the person who is reading. From now on, only the person who is holding the object can speak. The other partner is simply to listen. Later, the pillow will be passed and the other partner will have a turn at uninterrupted sharing.

Instructions for Listener: It is extremely important that you listen without saying a word. You are not to agree, disagree, or defend yourself. During the course of this exercise, your partner will be making requests for changes in your behavior. All you must do during this exercise is hear what your partner wants. Do not interrupt or argue, even if you think your partner is being unfair. Understand that this is an exercise in understanding your partner. There is absolutely no need for you to change any behaviors that your partner will be requesting.

Instructions to Sharer: Share three things that you resent about your partner, and what you would like instead.

Example: *I resent that you don't spend more time with me on weekends, and I would like you to spend at least one full day or two half-days with me every weekend.*

Do not use a negative request, such as: *I would like it if you did not go golfing every weekend.* It does not let your partner know what you want.

Do not use more than three or four sentences for each resentment. When your three resentments have
*Continued*

been stated, pass the pillow and let your partner share while you listen silently.

After both of you have shared three resentments, pass the pillow again, and each share three things that you appreciate about your partner.

---

This exercise is, in a sense, a good model to use in arguments. If each of you can merely hear the other person's point of view without having to respond or defend, it would greatly reduce the tendency to escalate a power struggle.

> *"The worst policy of all is to besiege walled cities."*
> —Sun Tzu

# Blaming

It is doubtful you truly believe that most of the problems in your marriage are your fault. You look at your spouse's behavior through *your* eyes, interpret his or her actions through *your* value system, and process it all through *your* brain. The whole process is filtered through *your* frame of reference. You are not exactly an unbiased observer. Even if you ask for an "unbiased" opinion from a friend or family member you are certainly more likely to pick someone sympathetic to your point of view, and that person is likely to render an opinion based on the facts that you provided through your perspective. Inevitably your conclusion is confirmed: your partner is the one who needs to do most of the changing.

Sometimes you may graciously assume 20, 30, or even 50 percent of the responsibility, but even that is not enough. If you accept half of the responsibility for a marital conflict, you will have a tendency to **blame** your partner for the other 50 percent, and consequently a considerable portion of your effort will go into trying to change your partner. Even when someone says: *"I will*

*accept ninety percent of the responsibility,"* it is usually
followed by a *"but . . ."* This usually translates into: *"I
will accept some of the responsibility, but **first** you must
admit and change your part of the problem."*

As each of you try to place the blame and coerce each
other into changing, you meet nothing but resistance.
Each waits for the other to make the first constructive
move, while the relationship remains in a destructive
standoff. Occasionally you may attempt some changes,
either because you are in a conciliatory mood or because you wish to confirm your expectation that your
partner never did have any intention of changing, no
matter what improvements you made. However, if your
partner corroborates your pessimistic expectation by not
responding with a corresponding change, you quickly
revert to your old behavior.

To bring change to your marriage, you must regard
any problems **as if** they are entirely your responsibility.
This does not mean that you must consider them your
fault. It simply means that you are the only one who can
modify your behavior, and your partner is the only one
who can alter his or hers. No matter how subtle, clever,
or brutal your attempts are to change your partner, they
will be met with resistance. You will never convince your
partner that he or she is the one who needs to make the
primary adjustments. That is human nature. Ultimately,
you must pursue self-insight and self-improvement, in-
dependent of whether your partner modifies his/her behavior.

Ironically, if you choose to point a finger and vow to
wait until your partner makes the first move before you
begin to work on your end of the relationship, you will
feel powerless. You are locked into a position where you
are dependent on your partner's actions before you can
affect any change in the relationship. Until your mate
makes the first move, you are helpless. You have re-

signed your control. If, on the other hand, you take personal responsibility, you can begin to initiate changes,
**with or without your spouse's cooperation.** That is a
major step in the right direction.

---

### EXERCISE 21

Write a list of three things on a sheet of paper that
you believe your partner would like to see change in
your marriage. Now take a separate piece of paper
and write a letter to yourself, from your partner,
blaming you for those three things and demanding
that you change. Be as negative as you can be, and be
sure to place the blame squarely on yourself. When
you have completed this, sit in a quiet place and read
the letter to yourself. Imagine how you would react if
your partner placed the blame squarely on your
shoulders. How would you defend yourself?

---

Obviously, the point of this exercise is to teach you
how uncomfortable it feels to be blamed and how destructive it is to your relationship. Accusations of this
type just serve to inflame marital conflicts.

# *Judgments*

Imagine for a second the imposing figure of a judge behind his raised courtroom desk, in his black robe and gavel in hand. You, the defendant, are standing in front of him, pleading your case. Even if you are convinced of your innocence, judges and courtrooms are intimidating. The same feeling of intimidation is what you encourage every time you act as a judge for your partner's actions or opinions. Judgment is a form of intimidation.

You and your partner both have different opinions and biases. Most of us believe that our opinions are correct. That is why we value them and hold on to them. If we believed our biases were not correct, we would change them. However, when opinions are transformed into judgments and then used as weapons, they become destructive to the relationship.

An opinion is a point of view based upon our personal reality. It does not automatically degrade opinions to the contrary. You and I can hold differing views on politics, abortion, or religion. I may not agree with you, but still I respect your right to a differing opinion. On the other hand, a judgment involves grading or evaluat-

ng another person's opinion, action, or belief. It puts
one opinion, and often one person, above the other.

Too frequently when we are embroiled in a disagreement, we become so convinced of the righteousness of
our own position that we critically conclude that actions
or statements of our partners are less worthy. That is a
judgment, and judgment in a marriage, or in any relationship for that matter, can be a very powerful weapon.

By judging your mate you are placing yourself in a
superior position. Inevitably, your partner will instinctively act self-protective. This may involve closing down
or counterattacking, but it will certainly not promote
opening up and becoming more vulnerable.

A particularly destructive "game" many couples encounter is one in which each person is convinced that
his perception of a problem is the right one and therefore his spouse's view is incorrect. The topic may range
from one as impersonal as world politics to one as intimate as how often to engage in sex, but the format of
the disagreement is usually the same. One (or often
both) of the combatants hurls around phrases or implications such as "I'm right," "You're wrong," "You're
crazy," "That's abnormal," or in some other way demeans the other, failing to take into consideration that
what is being expressed is a personal perception based
upon a unique filtering of the world. Whenever you
hear yourself or your partner using words like *good-bad,
normal-abnormal,* or even *right-wrong,* it is a tip-off that
the conversation is crossing the line from constructive
discussion into the area of critical judgment.

For example, a husband has come home late for the
third straight evening. Imagine that from his viewpoint
he is working hard because his boss is all over him to get
a report out by the end of the week. He is tired, angry at
having to work late, and just wants to get home. Imagine from the wife's viewpoint that during her first mar-

riage, her ex-husband ran off with the secretary. Now she is scared and is feeling jealous. He comes home tired, wanting to be left alone. Her experience is that he appears quiet, withdrawn, and uncommunicative. His experience is that his wife appears suspicious, asks a lot of questions, and wants to talk. He feels overwhelmed and suffocated. A fight ensues. Who is right and who is wrong? Each has responded to his or her own reality.

| HIS REALITY | HER REALITY |
|---|---|
| Working hard | First husband ran off |
| Pressure from boss/report due | Feeling jealous |
| Tired/wants to be left alone | He appears withdrawn |
| Feeling self protective | Feels rejected |
| She appears suspicious | Is suspicious |
| Feels suffocated | Wants to talk |

Even when you vehemently disagree with your spouse's opinion, it is important that you still respect his/her right to differ. The key is to listen. If you effectively listen to your partner and can acknowledge that you understand his/her differing position before presenting your own position, your partner will be more inclined to give you the same courtesy. If you attack your partner and/or his/her opinion, then you can expect either withdrawal or a counterattack.

This does not mean you must always agree. It simply means that it is not your job to judge whether your partner is right or wrong, but to share your perceptions and feelings and to understand your partner's. Your partner's opinion is as valid as yours, even though you may vigorously disagree. If you are worried about winning or losing in your marriage, there is no way you can maintain an effective discussion. To communicate effectively you must be willing to hear what the other person says, without any judgments. The following are two more rules to add to your communication repertoire:

RULE 10: *Keep an open mind when listening to your partner's point of view, then reassess your own position, using all the information at your disposal.*

This doesn't mean you have to change your mind. It just means that after you gather information, be flexible enough to take a look at the whole picture before reestablishing a new position. If you do change your position, let your partner know about it.

RULE 11: *No matter how much you disagree with your partner, do not judge or ridicule his/her opinion. Accept his/her right to hold a differing belief. If you wish to share your differing opinion, first clarify what you understand your partner to be saying. Let your mate know that you accept it as his/her opinion. Then, share your own belief.*

If one of you wins an argument, it means the other has lost. Inevitably, the defeated partner either escalates the conflict a notch, in hopes of reaffirming a victory, or withdraws and doesn't try at all. This promotes a constant power struggle, with the two of you assuming the roles of adversaries, rather than teammates working toward common goals.

Your perception of the world, and the set of values and opinions that you adopt as your own, are not equally valid for others. You may not agree with your spouse, but it is important that you respect that he/she may have a different viewpoint, based upon a unique set of life experiences. Your spouse's viewpoint is different —not superior, not inferior, just different.

If you are worried about winning or losing in a con
versation, there is no way you can be an effective lis
tener. To listen effectively you must be willing to hear
what the other person says, without any judgments. A
person who feels judged will act to protect him/herself
This may involve closing down or counterattacking, but
it will certainly not involve opening up and becoming
more vulnerable. Treat your mate in a way that indicates
acceptance and respect. This does not mean you must
always agree. It simply means you must recognize that
your partner's opinion is as valid as yours, even though
you may vigorously disagree.

The following assignment is to be done with your
partner. If you do not feel ready to approach your part
ner with the exercise, or your partner does not appear
willing to participate, an alternative is provided in ap
pendix E.

---

### EXERCISE 22

Pick a topic that the two of you have recently disagreed about or have argued about in the past. It
may even be one that is still being disagreed upon.
Stage a mock argument, with each of you playing the
role of the other. Try to choose similar arguments to
those your mate might pick, and act out his or her
mannerisms during an argument. Feel free to exaggerate. It often makes this type of role-playing more
fun.

After you have played out the argument, share
with each other how it felt to be in the other's shoes.

## DAY 23

# *Logic vs. Emotions*

One scenario that commonly elicits a great deal of judgment as to who is right and who is wrong is when one partner tends to be more emotional in a view of the world, and the other more logical. Typically, the logical partner acts like an attorney, placing into evidence a long string of arguments to back up his/her point of view, while the emotional partner defensively points to an inner feeling. Sometimes, in desperation, the emotional partner will try to piece together some logical arguments of his/her own but is usually outgunned.

This is not a fair fight. Logic and emotion are two completely different planes of perspective. Let's say that you and your marital partner go shopping for a car and you spot a beautiful little sports model. It's got all the bells and whistles you love. All you need to do is convince your partner. So you put together this wonderful logical argument: *"It's the right size, it's within the price range we agreed on, it's the color we said we wanted, and it has all the accessories we were looking for."*

Very logical, and well put. But your partner says: *"I don't want that one, it is not what I had in mind. I'll know*

123

*what I'm looking for when I see it."* A good emotional reply, based simply on an inner feeling—not logic. There is no place to go with the argument. Logically, the car fits your needs. Emotionally, it doesn't fit your partner's needs. End of argument! What is the difference whether there are a hundred logical reasons. If it doesn't fit both your needs, one will remain unhappy with the decision.

Frequently what occurs with couples when one is significantly more emotional and the other more logical is that the logical partner tends to look down on the reasoning of the emotional partner. He/she feels that anyone who cannot come up with hard evidence to back a position is inferior, or at least his/her argument is inferior. What this logical partner fails to appreciate is that for many decisions, an inner feeling is as valid a reason to choose a certain alternative as is logic. Emotion is not an inferior reason for making decisions, nor is it a superior reason, it simply involves different criteria than logic.

The use of logic is overrated in decision making. Even the most logical people frequently base their personal decisions on emotional reasons. However, when pressed as to why the decision was made, they give a logical justification. For example, probably the most important decision you make concerning your health is in choosing your personal physician. Do you have any idea what medical school your doctor went to, or what your doctor's class ranking was? Do you have any idea how well thought of the doctor is by colleagues? Most likely the decisions you made in choosing your physician were based primarily upon his/her personality. That is an emotional, gut-feeling decision. If asked to defend why you use that doctor you will most likely give logical reasons (e.g., he certainly has always been right in the past, or John Jones recommended her), but again, that choice is frequently made intuitively—based upon emotions. You like your physician's manner and trust him or her as a person.

No matter which side of this logical/emotional fence you sit on, it is imperative that you respect your partner's decision making. That does not mean you must change your opinion, or even your way of making decisions. Nor does it mean that you need to agree with your partner. It simply means that you must respect your partner's right to hold a differing opinion and not spend your time battering him/her into agreeing with you.

The following exercise can help you begin to experience your disagreements as information-gathering sessions rather than adversarial encounters.

---

### EXERCISE 23

Sit down with your partner or a friend and discuss a topic that has been an area of disagreement between the two of you. No matter what your partner shares, your only response must be *"I would like you to share more"* or *"I appreciate your input."*

If you feel that you and your partner can handle the challenge, repeat the exercise, but this time, every time he or she brings up a point you disagree with, challenge it. Notice the difference between the two ways of disagreeing.

---

# Constructive Disagreement

As the winds of change blow through your marriage and both you and your mate view life through your personal kaleidoscopes, the differences between your unique perspectives will inevitably lead to some disagreements. But disagreement need not be about fighting and distancing yourself. The object of this chapter is to teach you how to use differences in a constructive way, as a tool for building greater trust and intimacy in your relationship.

If you have experienced difficulties with fighting and arguing during your marriage, the concept of disagreeing in a constructive manner must seem like a contradiction of terms. However, it is a learnable skill, well within your grasp. In a constructive disagreement there need not be any major battles or adversarial positions, and each of you can retain your personal point of view. Instead of being viewed as "a disaster waiting to happen," you can turn disagreements into a forum for expressing your needs and learning more about your partner's perspective.

There is an old saying: *"If you're not a part of the solution, you're part of the problem."* No place is this more true than in a marital conflict. Either the two of you are on the same team or you are not. To resolve conflicts constructively in your relationship you must join your spouse as a **teammate.** This does not mean you always have to agree with your partner, nor does it mean you consistently have to acquiesce. It simply signifies that you are consistently willing to handle conflicts with a constructive intent and treat your partner as a respected equal. Your commitment as a teammate is to work toward resolution of the conflict. There must be no *put downs,* no demeaning statements, and no physical, verbal, or emotional abuse.

It is interesting to watch couples progress during marital counseling. Often they wrestle for weeks or months, locked in a battle—each trying to win, or at least avoid losing. They act like two children, each trying to pin the blame on the other. Then a change becomes apparent in counseling. Both begin to take the rules of effective communication seriously. The blaming disappears and each assumes personal responsibility for his or her own actions. They become teammates. Even though their skill at resolving conflicts may still be rudimentary, their change in attitude foreshadows a positive shift for the relationship.

## When to Disagree

For a variety of reasons, all of us at some time avoid disagreements. Maybe you judge the circumstances to be wrong for a deep or lengthy personal discussion, or you are too overwhelmed to face one more pressure. Other times, you may be so angry or upset that acting like a cooperative teammate is the last thing on your mind. Ideally, however, the best time to deal with a conflict is immediately, when you first become aware of it. Don't give the disagreements a chance to accumulate and fester into deeper resentments. As soon as you realize that you are holding back a difference, bring it into the open. When a disagreement gets skirted, your relationship may appear harmonious on the surface, but within your body tension builds and eventually gets expressed in covert ways.

Following is a remark made by the actress Marlo Thomas in regard to her relationships with her mother and her celebrity husband, Phil Donahue:

> If I talk to my mother and she sounds kind of funny on the other end, I call her back and say, "Okay, what is it? What did I do?" I've got to get the tension cleared up, apologize if I was wrong, protest if I was hurt, or it sticks in my brain and bothers me and colors all my emotions. I think Phil was more reticent about expressing his feelings before he met me. But now he gets it out, too. He says what's on his mind. That means that we argue when we need to, but it also means that we don't harbor grievances. The air between us is sometimes loud and stormy, but it always clears.*

Constructive disagreement is a form of intimacy. It communicates to your partner. *I trust you enough to share with you how deeply this conflict affects me.* If you are afraid to honestly communicate your differences, it indicates a lack of trust in your partner. The avoidance may reflect a feeling that your mate is not strong enough to handle a confrontation or a fear that he or she will not love you if you disagree. It may even be representative of a fear that your partner will use the differences as an opportunity to physically or emotionally batter you or, even abandon you. Whatever your

* "Marlo Talks About Marriage, Romance, and Phil," Susan Dworkin, *Ladies Home Journal,* May 1983, p 24.

reason, if you bury your differences without comment, your mate will be left to interpret or misinterpret your feelings and wants based solely on your facial expressions, gestures, tone of voice, and indirect verbalizations.

## The Art of Constructive Disagreement

Since the object of resolving conflict is to understand your partner's point of view and to convey your own, your ability to communicate effectively is of critical importance. If you are busy defending yourself or counter-attacking, you will not fully digest what your partner is trying to express. The conflict will remain unresolved and differences will continue, but on a silent level. Consequently, the cornerstone of constructive disagreement is the eleven commandments of effective communication presented in the preceding chapters. A list of these rules are contained in Appendix F.

To engage in a truly constructive disagreement assumes not only that you have mastered all of these rules, but that you are willing to comply with them. The first part, mastering the rules, is essentially a matter of practice. However, complying with the rules is not always a simple matter, especially during the heat of a battle. Sometimes during a disagreement you feel so hurt or angry that your immediate instinct is to seek revenge or to retreat. At a time like this, it is difficult to forgo these destructive impulses and attempt a peaceful resolution.

The following is a good example of how one married couple became entrapped in a destructive pattern and how the self-protective walls they erected actually escalated the conflict:

*Shana was a thirty-six-year-old woman who came from a family where she was ignored and felt unloved. Mark, forty-one, came from a similar background. Each needed a great deal of love, but both were afraid of committing to the relationship because they feared the other would be rejecting. Frequently they would have fights that would blow them apart for days. Each was about ready to welcome divorce as the easy way out when, in the course of marital counseling, they discovered that they were unknowingly engaged in some interesting and destructive patterns of communication. Notice how each person's actions served to inflame the situation and escalate the level of conflict.*

1. *When they would disagree about any subject, even a relatively minor one, Shana was always more vocal and considerably louder.*
2. *Mark, knowing that it was fruitless to attempt to outshout what he perceived as a verbal attack by Shana, protected himself by sitting quietly, pretending to listen, all the time smiling impassively.*
3. *Feeling that the smiling was a demeaning gesture by Mark, Shana would escalate her assault by calling Mark insulting names.*
4. *Again, seeking to defend himself, Mark counterattacked by raising issues that he knew Shana was extremely sensitive about, such as her abilities as a mother.*
5. *Occasionally, the battle would conclude with one or the other shoving, slapping, or in some way physically attacking the other.*

This is communication run amuck! This couple has managed to turn a relatively minor disagreement into World War III. Not because of a lack of love or caring but because each, in an effort to protect him/herself, unthinkingly escalated the conflict. Both participants departed with a feeling of anger and distrust, and neither had any sense of resolution.

## Disagreeing About Decisions

There is no requirement that couples who are married must think or act with uniformity. There will be times when the two of you can **agree to disagree,** and each can act independently. When this occurs, respect your partner's right to hold a differing opinion, and follow the eleven rules of effective communication until both of you feel the issue has been resolved.

> *Pete and Ronni were invited to Pete's nephew's wedding. Although Pete wanted to get tickets for them to fly to Phoenix for the wedding, Ronni objected. She did not like Pete's nephew and did not want to spend their money to see him get married. Pete, on the other hand, wanted to be present at this family celebration. After discussing the issues thoroughly, both remained firm in their respective points of view. Consequently, Pete chose to attend the wedding and Ronni chose to stay at home. They resolved the issue by each acting independently.*

The processes of sharing and listening are wonderful tools for negotiating differences, but sometimes a single action, or compromise, is called for. This might occur if the two of you disagree about where to go on vacation or disagree about whether or not to have a child. **This does not mean that either of you necessarily has to alter your convictions.** The only compromise that needs to take place is in the action taken. Each of you has a right to retain your differing opinion.

If you choose to accept your partner's solution, do not sulk or hold your partner responsible for the decision. Likewise, do not become a martyr or batter him or her with resentment for not doing things your way. You made the choice to join your spouse in that decision, and you, too, must now accept responsibility for it. If the results of the decision do not turn out positively, do not use this as an opportunity to say *I told you so.* You were an equal partner in that decision.

When it is your partner who relents on the decision, do not use this as an excuse to celebrate a victory. If you act as if you have gained a major victory, your partner will likely feel as if he or she has suffered a serious defeat. Appreciate that he has relinquished his first choice and empathically understand and acknowledge any loss or pain that he or she feels as a result of giving in. Again, recognize that you and your spouse are on the same team.

Example: *I really appreciate that you are willing to postpone the decision to have a baby for a year. I understand how much you would like to be a mother, but I really feel like I am under too much pressure to be a good father.*

You and your spouse will always see the world through your unique perspectives, and therefore will never form a mythical union, free of difficulties and conflict. Disagreements are often an opportunity for understanding, rather than an invitation for disaster—a chance to explore the differences between you and to learn about your partner's wants, values, beliefs, and feelings. There is no difference too trivial to confront. Likewise, there is no disagreement of such magnitude that your partner needs to be shielded from your feelings. If you choose not to air your differences, you and your mate lose an opportunity to understand each other's perspectives and to discuss and resolve differences. And more important, you miss a chance at intimacy.

### EXERCISE 24

Pick the communication rule that you have been experiencing the greatest problem with, and continue to break it (The rules are listed in Appendix A). Every time you break it, notice the reaction of the person with whom you are conversing.

Does he/she become defensive? Argumentative? Does the conversation flow like any normal conversation?

## DAY 25

## *Abusive Disagreements*

Few people consider themselves as abusive or abused in a marriage. Nevertheless, if you consider the wider definition of abuse, there are times in all our marriages when we have felt mistreated, and there are times when our mates have perceived us as being abusive.

Abuse in relationships is not always obvious. Most people recognize physical violence, verbal threats, intimidation, or obviously demeaning remarks as forms of abuse. However, it is the subtle forms that often go unnoticed. Criticism, judgments, repeated verbal floggings for a past indiscretion, and even something as simple as name-calling are forms of abuse. Included in the latter category are not only the obviously abusive names—bitch, bastard, SOB, etc.,—but names to hurt or stereotype—cold, rigid, just like your mother, etc. Other times the abuse is meted out as cold silence or calculated neglect.

These human violations frequently become so ingrained as a part of the daily routine that neither person ever identifies them as abuse. They become tolerated as acceptable ingredients in the marital interaction.

*Joan was in her sixth year of her second marriage. Her first husband, Ted, had left her and their two sons suddenly after twelve years of what Joan had thought was a fairly decent relationship. John, her second husband, worked hard at his job as an accountant, and for the most part treated her and the children well. However, every time Joan would verbalize a complaint, John refused to talk about it. If Joan persisted in her efforts, John threatened to leave Joan and the boys.*

*John knew that divorce was a very vulnerable area for Joan, and he counted on his threats as a way of closing off the discussion. His intent was not to solve the problem, but to shut down the communication through the use of intimidation. Neither partner recognized it as abuse, nor did John intend it as abuse. It was simply his way of defending himself. Nonetheless, John was abusing Joan in a very subtle way.*

There can be no excuse for abuse in a relationship. Whether it occurs by design or is unintentional, and whether the offending partner is intoxicated or sober, abuse is a violation of the spirit of marriage. Apologies and excuses do not erase the scars, nor do they lessen the emotional impact of the abuse. When either partner feels abused, effective communication ceases and fear and/or revenge become the driving forces in the relationship.

### Dealing with a Hostile or Uncooperative Partner

Even if you scrupulously adhere to the rules recommended in this book and work toward resolving a conflict, that does not ensure that your partner will reciprocate. If your mate acts hostile or uncooperative during a disagreement, it may still be possible to keep the disagreement flowing in a positive direction. To do this:

Share your feelings;
State whatever boundaries you need to protect
   yourself;
Clarify what you would like from your partner; and
Continue to follow all eleven rules, even when your
   partner does not.

Here is an example:

PARTNER 1 *(employing the eleven rules): I feel lonely to-night. I would like you to be more attentive to me.*
HOSTILE PARTNER *(pointing in Partner 1's face): All you do is complain. You can be such an SOB sometimes. I don't know why I stay in this marriage. I ought to leave.*
PARTNER 1: *Please stop waving your finger in my face and threatening to leave* (Boundary). *I feel scared and angry when you do that* (Feeling). *I was simply trying to let you know what I want* (Clarification).

If you state a boundary and your partner does not respect it, clearly restate it. This is especially helpful if the other person was not paying attention to your boundary, or for some reason did not take it seriously. If in the preceding example, the hostile partner continued to be abusive, Partner 1 might just repeat: *I feel scared and angry when you wave your finger at me or threaten to leave* (Feeling). *I feel like I did when I was a child. I was simply trying to let you know what I want* (Clarification). *I would appreciate if you would just listen to me without waving your finger or threatening to leave* (Boundary).

Under no circumstances should you allow your boundaries to be trampled. Nor should you allow yourself to get sucked into an argument or retaliate in any way. If your limit repeatedly is not respected, simply reiterate the same boundary again and again.

If that does not work, then you will have to add consequences to your limits. These should not be consequences designed to punish your partner, but rather consequences designed to protect yourself: *"If you cross my boundary then I'm going to . . ."* You are letting your spouse know that there are consequences contingent upon his or her actions. What you are doing is clarifying what your boundaries are and letting your partner choose whether to bear the consequences.

Example: *Unless you are willing to go for marital counseling, I feel like I can no longer continue in this relationship.*

Issuing any contingency is a very serious action to take and can have a dramatic impact on your relationship. If you make a statement of what the consequences will be for breaching your boundary, make sure you follow through with the promised consequences. Never issue idle threats. Otherwise you will weaken your believability for any future limits that you set.

### Dealing with Explosiveness; Your Partner's or Your Own

Even if your partner acts explosively or emotionally abusive, it is still possible to follow the eleven rules. Just firmly set your boundary. Tell your partner that you are leaving the room, the house, etc., and that you need some time until things calm down. This may be a frightening task with a partner who appears out of control, but the alternative is to remain terrified and intimidated. If you want to become an equal member of the team, you must feel secure in your own limits. Specify a time when you will return to talk. If your partner pursues you as you are leaving, repeat yourself. Do not engage in defensiveness, and do not return the abusiveness. This will only further inflame the situation. If your partner becomes physically assaultive, immediately leave and call the police. Under circumstances where you seriously fear a physical assault, give serious consideration to not returning until steps are taken to assure you of your physical safety. These steps should definitely include counseling for your partner, yourself, and/or the two of you conjointly.

If it is your own explosiveness you are concerned about, likewise explain to your partner that you need time to calm down, and be specific about what time you will return to discuss the matter. Do not just flee without giving your partner a timetable. If you do, your partner will likely be concerned that the issue will not be resolved, and may pursue you. If your partner continues to follow in spite of your protests and warnings, just leave and come back when you feel able to enter into an open discussion.

Whether you identify yourself as abused or not, there are specific steps you can take to identify and minimize hurtful situations. The following exercise will help you to become more aware of painful or abusive behaviors that exist in your marriage.

---

### EXERCISE 25

Write in your notebook what you consider to be abuses or hurtful situations that you have experienced with your partner.
Examples:

*I feel like you abuse me by calling me names.*
*I feel like you treat my opinions as if they are unimportant.*

*Continued*

I feel very scared and intimidated when you
seem out of control when you get angry.

Now, close your eyes and anticipate what it would
be like if you share your hurt with your mate. (If you
trust your mate enough to share these situations, find
a time when the two of you can comfortably talk and
share all of your feelings. If your memories include
any memories of abuse from childhood or other
times in your life, consider them as well.)

If just anticipating a dialogue with your partner about
the issues you just wrote down raises fear or anxiety
inside of you, then you might be suffering serious
wounds from a previous hurt or abuse. The origin of
these injuries may stem from your present marriage,
your relationship with one or both parents, or from
some other painful relationship in your life. Recognizing these wounds is an important step toward resolving
them, and toward establishing an atmosphere that is
more conducive to constructive disagreements in your
current relationship.

# Sexual Compatibility

All couples are sexually incompatible, at least to some degree. You and your partner are unique individuals, and that uniqueness extends to your capacity to express your sexuality. Included in the sexual differences that distinguish the two of you are your sexual drive, sexual interest, willingness to be exploratory and innovative, attraction toward your partner, willingness to take the initiative, sexual enthusiasm, and the importance sex plays in your life. Yet, in spite of all of these predictable differences, many couples seem to become concerned when they perceive the slightest gap in their sexual compatibility.

Not only is your unique sexual makeup different from your partner's, but in a sense it is different than it was even one day ago. The ongoing events of your world change your sexuality almost on a moment-to-moment basis. At any given instant, it has the potential to be affected by numerous variables, including the following:

**Genetic.** The most obvious difference between you and your mate has to do with gender. Generally, men and women approach sex with somewhat different outlooks. Men often consider sex to be a sign of their masculinity or virility and seem to place considerable emphasis on orgasm and erection. This emphasis on performance tends to make men especially vulnerable to sexual performance pressure and sexual dysfunction. Many women, on the other hand, tend to view sex as a sign of how much they are loved or cherished. Their need is more in the direction of intimacy and tenderness.

**Psychological.** All of us have a general psychological state that defines who we are: a sense of confidence in ourselves, a feeling of self-esteem, an overall mood, and a personality which is distinctive to all who know us. But along with these more obvious traits are such variables as inhibitions, fears, special feelings about our bodies, all of which form a foundation upon which our sexual self is built.

Layered on top of this general psychological state, our feelings shift every day, even from moment to moment. These fluctuations affect our interest and ability to operate sexually. Sometimes the reasons for these changes are obvious: grieving due to a death, celebration of a promotion, anxiety due to work and family pressures—but sometimes they occur for no obvious reason. One psychological state that has an especially devastating effect on sexual experiences is *performance anxiety*—the tendency for a person to become so concerned about performance during a sexual experience that tension builds and he/she misses the enjoyment of the moment.

**Couple and Family.** Everything that happens between you and your mate effects your sexuality. Every family crisis, every vacation, the power struggles, the times of suppressed or expressed anger, and the moments when you resolve your differences and feel intimate. All have the power to change how you respond sexually.

**Physiological.** Anything that alters your body chemistry has the potential to affect your sexuality. This includes illness, pregnancy, medications, and other chemical agents absorbed into the body. Even the simplest cold can alter your sex drive. However, the illnesses that are most likely to make a lasting impact are chronic illnesses.

The drugs used to treat many maladies sometimes have side effects that affect sexuality. This includes over-the-counter medications. Check with your physician if you suspect some medicine may be affecting you. Also, consider how your sexuality may be affected by the use of tobacco and alcohol. Both have been shown to have very significant effects.

**Previous Learning.** Every experience, sexual and otherwise, that you have had in prior relationships or in your marriage, is recorded on your personal kaleidoscope. Some of these continue to affect your perception of yourself, your body, the opposite sex, and virtually every aspect of the sexual experience. The education you received as a child, the taboos drummed into your head, and the encouraging messages of family, friends, and prior lovers, all have become a part of your sexual being.

**Trauma.** Rapes, molestation experiences, or other traumas effect your sexual being, your ability to trust, and your ability to be intimate with another person. Whether the trauma occurred only once and lasted briefly, or whether it was experienced over a long period of time, may have a significant impact on your sexuality.

**Aging.** Because the process is so gradual, we hardly notice the changes that aging brings to our sexuality. Yet physically your body is different now than it was when you first began having sexual relationships. Although our bodies are constantly undergoing these physical changes, there is no reason why couples cannot maintain a relatively active sexual relationship throughout their lives.

**Culture.** As we have previously discussed, our culture gives us conflicting messages about sex. On the one hand, sex is openly used to seduce us into buying various products, while on the other, educational information about sex is reduced to a trickle in the public media. This schizophrenic message plays on all of our minds. For the rebellious it can act as a trumpet call to sexual action, while for others it may act as a source of shame, discouraging comfortable sexuality.

Religion and ethnic origin also play a role in the way we perceive our sexuality. Some religious and ethnic groups openly dissuade their followers from engaging in sexual contact as a source of intimacy or enjoyment, while others are much more encouraging.

Our culture is also a cradle for destructive myths, many of which affect the way we perceive sexuality or respond to it. Myths proliferate about masturbation, the size of men's penises, AIDS, the importance of orgasm, and a host of other topics.

Whether sex in your marriage has been extremely compatible or a constant struggle, one thing is clear: you and your partner have different sexual needs, wants, and beliefs. Avoid judging who is right and who is wrong. The two of you are simply looking at a very complex issue through two extremely different kaleidoscopes.

## Sexual Dysfunction

For many couples, sex becomes a source of considerable discomfort and pain. All of us have experienced times when sex doesn't work quite right. That is to be expected, and it is nothing to worry about. Often these difficulties are eliminated when marital or life stresses are eliminated, or after the couple has an open airing of the problem. However, as soon as you recognize that sex has become work or a source of continuing tension for either you or your mate, it is time to consider some intervention. If left to ferment, sexual problems have the potential to undermine the confidence of individuals and the foundations of marriages. More than half of the couples in this country will experience a sexual problem at some point in their marriage that is serious enough to warrant professional help.

The following are the most commonly experienced sexual dysfunctions:

**Premature ejaculation.** The male ejaculates before or soon after the penis enters the vagina, interfering with the satisfaction of one or both partners.

**Failure to reach orgasm.** Occurring in both men and women, this happens despite a feeling of arousal.

**Lack of arousal.** This also occurs in both men and women and may happen despite the fact that the person maintains an interest in sex.

**Discrepancies in interest.** One partner has a considerably different level of interest in sex than the other.

**Erectile problems.** Men with this problem consistently find it difficult to attain or maintain an erection sufficient to complete intercourse.

**Painful intercourse.** This is far more frequent in women than men but does occur in both genders. Although this is frequently due to psychological reasons, it should first be checked out by a physician.

Many couples make a serious mistake by delaying treatment for years because of embarrassment or the false hope that the problem will work out on its own. This is highly unlikely. Once a sexual problem becomes entrenched, it is difficult to treat without professional assistance. Often what one or both partners will do in an attempt to resolve their sexual difficulties, is *work* at solving the problem. Unfortunately, *work* is counterproductive to sexual arousal. People do not get sexually aroused when they are working at something. Consequently, the dysfunction worsens.

If both partners are motivated and open to treatment, sexual dysfunctions are readily reversible. Usually both partners are treated, because each is in his/her own way actively involved in the problem. Most mental health professionals are **not** sufficiently expert in this area to treat a sexual dysfunction. Seek counseling with a **certified sex therapist.** If you have difficulty locating a certified sex therapist, write to the American Association of Sex Educators, Counselors, and Therapists (AASECT), 435 North Michigan Avenue, Chicago, IL 60611.

---

### EXERCISE 26

The following questions will help you identify some of the feelings you have about sex and what pieces may be missing from your sexual relationship. After you finish writing the answers to these questions feel free to communicate them to your partner. If your decision is not to share the answers with your partner, answer one additional question: I choose not to share openly with my partner about sex because . . .

1. What I like best about our sexual encounters is . . .
2. What I like least about our sexual encounters is . . .
3. What I most enjoy sexually about my partner is . . .

*Continued*

4. What I am most afraid to tell my partner about my sexuality is . . .
5. What I believe my partner truly thinks about my body is . . .
6. My feeling about my body is . . .
7. While I was growing up, sex in my family was . . .
8. What I learned about sex from my religion was . . .
9. The way I feel about my partner's body is . . .
10. What I would like to add to our sexual repertoire is . . .
11. Masturbating in front of my partner is . . .
12. What I sexually fantasize most about is . . .
13. The way I feel about sharing my sexual fantasies with my partner is . . .

# *Making Decisions*

For many of our grandparents, the process of marital decision making was relatively simple. Whenever there was a difference of opinion, ultimately it was the man who decided the final outcome. Like a reigning king, he could decide whether or not to get input from his "subjects" before declaring the final edict.

The active participation of women in decision making is a relatively new concept in our culture. In a monarchy, where a single person rules, the decision-making procedure is simple. However, the democratic system is fairer, though far more complicated. Everyone gets a single vote, and the rule of the majority determines the ultimate decision.

In a sense, marriage is a dreadful democracy—a democracy with only two votes. If both people vote for decision A, or both for decision B, everything functions smoothly. But frequently in a two-vote democracy the vote becomes deadlocked, with each partner opting for a different decision. In those situations, only two outcomes are possible. Either there is compromise or there is conflict.

This decision-making process in your marriage is further complicated by the incredible complexity of life in our generation. Our grandparents lived in a world of far fewer options. They did not face hundreds of competing consumer items or slick advertisements subtly trying to influence their choice of those products. Nor did they confront business pressures complicated by reams of computer information or demands for instant decisions over a telephone or fax.

In our modern society, everything we do involves hundreds of options—where we eat, where we vacation, how we keep our children from getting involved in drugs. The number of alternatives offered to our grandparents was limited by the size of the world they lived in and the amount of information available to them. Their world was local. Ours is global. Their information was limited by their curiosity and the few books and newspapers they had time to read. Ours is force-fed to us over television, radio, computers, magazines, newspapers, and easily available books on any topic of interest. The sheer number of decisions that we make on a daily basis, multiplied by the mind-boggling number of alternatives to choose from, gives us an equation that complicates our marriages immensely. There is no time for balloting on every issue, and often there is little time for discussion and negotiation.

When our grandparents faced marital conflicts they did not have the confusing options presented by separation, divorce, professional counseling, self-help books, or call-in radio gurus. Their decisions were no doubt as crucial to them as ours seem to us, but their pressures were primarily due to a lack of options rather than an abundance.

## Legal and Verbal Contracts

To facilitate the decision-making process, you and your mate have unknowingly established a series of unwritten and frequently unspoken agreements governing the daily chores and routine of your relationship. The two of you have established **contracts,** which determine who sleeps on which side of the bed, who stays home with the children, who shops for the groceries, and what would happen if one partner had an extramarital relationship. These agreements govern the simple trivialities of your relationship as well as the gut-wrenching crises. They are the laws that bring order to your relationship and regulate the everyday decisions.

The most obvious contract involved in your marriage is the one you agreed to the moment you said "I do." The marital vows you affirmed and the written certificate you signed combine to form an agreement that is enforceable by law. Few people remember the essence of the vows that bound them together at the time they were married. They may remember such words as *for richer or poorer,* or *till death do us part,* but few seem to recognize these marital vows as more than a ceremonial ritual. In the actual day-to-day running of a marriage, the legal marital contract has little conscious impact. The certificate remains tucked away in a drawer or vault, with little thought of its legal implications. Only when one or both of the partners consider changing the status of the contract, through separation, divorce, or annulment, do the legal nuances of that agreement get closely scrutinized.

Those legally binding vows were only the first and the most obvious of many contracts that presently guide your marriage. There are numerous **verbal contracts** that the two of you have negotiated over the length of your marriage. Each of you has verbally acknowledged that you are accountable for certain responsibilities that are required for the daily maintenance of the relationship. One of you has agreed to take primary responsibility for birth control measures, and one of you will take out the garbage every day. It is not necessary to have a daily debate as to who will be assigned these responsibilities. The two of you have also agreed to certain guidelines and goals for the marriage, such as the number of children you intend to have and who the breadwinner will be. Neither of you has signed any legal documents, but through discussions at one time or another, these issues have been agreed upon. They are verbal contracts.

---

### EXERCISE 27

List three things you have contractually agreed to in your marriage. Examples:

*I take out the garbage every day.*
*I drive the car when the two of us are together.*
*I cook the meals.*

Pick one of the three things on your list and imagine the process of negotiating a change with your partner.

---

The point of this exercise is that contracts in your marriage can be changed. Any verbal agreement can be altered by mutual consent, but you must take the first step by asking for what you want.

# Phantom Agreements

To survive in this rocket-paced world, it is not always possible to take the time to make marital decisions by written or verbal contract. Life circumstances change so rapidly there is no time for couples to discuss or preconsider every scenario imaginable. Consequently, to facilitate the decision-making process, couples set up a series of pacts, which are not written, not verbalized, and rarely acknowledged openly by either partner. They are agreements based upon meta-messages between the two of you. These **phantom agreements** are present in virtually every nook and cranny of your marriage, and in fact effect the bulk of your marital decisions. Because the signals these accords are based upon are often vague, these phantom agreements are open for a great deal of personal interpretation and distortion based upon each partner's personal frame of reference.

There are hundreds and even thousands of phantom agreements to which you and your partner have agreed. A few of the more obvious ones include:

1. How often you will have sex with your partner
2. Who will be more assertive in the relationship

3. The acceptability or non-acceptability of flirting or carrying on an extramarital relationship

Even though there has been no formal contract signed, violation of an implicit agreement can have a major effect on your marriage. If both partners, in their own nonverbal way, accept the terms of a phantom agreement, then a kind of contract exists. For example, if you and your spouse, without ever saying a word, agree that a certain amount of playful flirting is permissable for each of you, but extramarital relationships are not, then those terms become accepted as an **implicit contract** between the two of you. There is a general understanding as to what is expected from each, even though these issues have never been explicitly discussed.

*Kevin and Maria had been married three years. During that time, Kevin had been flirtatious on a few occasions, but Maria, feeling confident in their relationship, had viewed his flirtatiousness as harmless play. At a party one evening, Kevin's occasional attention and bantering with an attractive female guest was more than Maria could handle. Each time Kevin returned to toy verbally with the woman, Maria felt more hurt and angry. She waited until the party was over, and then as soon as the car door was closed, broke into tears. She felt violated. A little harmless flirting was okay as far as she was concerned, but she felt that his constant attention to the woman had violated the spirit of their marriage. Kevin, having felt that Maria had implicitly okayed his flirting on previous occasions was surprised that Maria was upset. Each understood the unspoken contract differently. From Maria's viewpoint the implicit contract they had about flirting had been breached. From Kevin's viewpoint it had not.*

**Maria**

Z

Father Had Affair
Feeling Unattractive
He Had Been Late Two Times
Feeling Jealous
Saw & Heard Closeness with Co-Worker

X

Never Chastised
Mother Never Intervened
Saw as Harmless Game
Bantering Part of Game
Two Drinks Lowered
Inhibitions

Y

**Kevin**

Kevin's frame of reference:

He had flirted previously, and not been chastised.

He had frequently seen his father flirting, and never saw his mother intervene.

He felt loving toward Maria. The *other woman* was a co-worker he frequently bantered with.

He had finished two drinks and was feeling play-
*Continued*

ful and uninhibited, and it was an innocent game which he had no intention of carrying any further.

Maria's frame of reference:

She saw Kevin being more physical and using sexual double entendres with his co-worker.

She had been feeling slightly jealous the past two weeks, because he had come home late on three occasions during that period of time.

She had put on a few pounds, and was feeling unattractive.

Her father had at one time had an affair with a co-worker, which nearly broke up the marriage between him and Maria's mother.

The obvious problem with implicit contracts is that they are vague and unstated. This adds to the probability that each partner will distort his viewpoint through the layers of his personal frame of reference. Again, each partner viewing the same situation (**X**) comes to a different understanding of the terms of the contract. Kevin interpreted the unspoken contract in one way (**Y**), and Maria interpreted it differently (**Z**).

This is what makes all phantom agreements so dangerous. Every phantom agreement is based upon the assumption that your mate has agreed to the same covenant. Yet, because these phantom agreements are so prone to personal distortions, and because the elements of time and changing circumstances add to this warping process, the potential for conflict is ever present. The lack of verbalization or direct confirmation between you and your mate greatly increases the potential for each to reach a different understanding of what is expected. The earlier figure represents misreadings that commonly occur as the result of phantom agreements. Both partners agreed to a contract, but each interpreted it somewhat differently.

Not all phantom agreements are agreed to by both partners. Sometimes a contract exists solely in the mind of one of the partners under the mistaken assumption that the other mate has agreed to the same terms. In that partner's mind a contract exists that is just as valid as if both partners had sat down and signed an agreement in blood. Any violation of this unilaterally distorted agreement is treated as a breach of the laws of the marriage, even though the other partner never agreed to the terms and conditions, and in fact was not even aware that any contract existed.

*Sam and Martha entered counseling because each felt let down and betrayed by the other. Sam had recently entered a business venture that had failed, using up all of their savings. If they were to keep their home, it was now necessary for both of them to work. Because of this, Martha felt betrayed and angry. She assumed that they both implicitly agreed when they were married that Sam would take care of her, just as her father had constantly provided for her mother. She understood that Sam's priority was that a mother's place was in the home, and she would be able to stay home to raise their two children.*

*Sam was never aware that this was Martha's understanding. Instead, his perception was that his wife would back him in any crisis. During times of financial difficulties in his family, his mother had intermittently filled in for missing employees at his father's factory and had worked for two years during especially lean times. He expected that now that he was in trouble, Martha would help out just as his mother did. Neither had previously mentioned their expectations to the other. Both incorrectly assumed a mutual contract existed. When each*

*violated the covenants of the contract that the other as-
sumed to be valid, feelings of betrayal followed.*

### Changing Contracts

You have engaged in thousands of personal and legal
contracts throughout your lifetime, with a multitude of
different people. Some of the contracts have been fulfilled, others have been violated, and many have expired
or been modified over the years. Few of those contracts
are still valid. Your life changes on a daily basis, and
consequently so does your marriage and your marital
contracts. Whether through evolution or revolution, all
contracts go through a constant process of change.
There is no such thing as maintaining a status quo in
your marriage. Transitions, crises, and even the relatively innocuous alterations to life, dictate that contracts
be updated to adjust to the varying assumptions under
which they are drawn. There is no way you can inhibit
those changes, any more than you can restrict the natural flow of the tides.

The key to renegotiating and clarifying personal contracts is effective communication. The more openly you
discuss your concerns and differences with your partner,
the fewer implicit contracts with which you will have to
contend. This process will reduce the amount of ambiguity in your relationship. Use the skills you have already learned, along with the lessons of the following
chapter, to help you resolve contractual differences between you and your partner and turn potential conflicts
into positive learning experiences.

The point of the following exercise is to demonstrate
how many agreements there are in your relationship
that the two of you have probably never even discussed.
And for every one listed is this exercise, there are likely
dozens of others.

## EXERCISE 28

Take a few moments and imagine how you and your spouse would react if . . .

1. all of a sudden your desire for sexual intercourse doubled or even tripled.
2. your partner no longer had any sexual desire.
3. the more assertive of the two of you lost confidence and suddenly stopped being assertive in the relationship.
4. you began to act very flirtatious with the opposite sex.
5. your spouse had a brief extramarital relationship.

# DAY 29

## *Adjusting to the Bumps*

Completing the first twenty-eight days of this program has provided you with a meaningful start toward improving your relationship, but even if you have faithfully carried out all the exercises and digested all the text, that still will not be sufficient to sustain your marital skills. The insights and principles you have acquired since beginning this program need to be expanded and built upon, and the skills you have learned need to be habitually practiced and honed, until all become a natural part of your repertoire. Improving your marriage requires a continual process of applying your newly acquired skills, evaluating the results, and then fine-tuning them the next time they are utilized. To maximize the effectiveness of this program, reread this book periodically, concentrating especially on those lessons and exercises that have been most difficult for you to master. This will help you to refresh your memory and your skills. When you misapply some of the skills you have learned, do not treat these "slips" as failures. They are important opportunities to learn—chances to notice what happens when you return to some of your old habits.

As you shift boundaries, adjust contracts, and abandon old rituals for new ones, the structure of your marriage will inevitably change. And, as is true of most newly learned behaviors, this change will often be accompanied by a feeling of awkwardness, as well as a host of emotions. At times you may feel the elation of a relationship seemingly being reborn, and at other times, you may experience the pain and fear that accompanies a marriage that feels as if it is falling apart.

It is our hope that the skills provided by this book have increased the harmony in your relationship. However, because the lessons of the past twenty-eight days may have encouraged you to scrutinize your marriage, the results may include a heightened awareness of your pain and your marital stress. If so, this is not necessarily an indication that you or your relationship is in danger. Your tension is merely a signal that your relationship is out of synch with your personal needs.

Often people who are aware of tension in their marriage fool themselves into believing that if they can maintain the status quo, their marital problems will eventually disappear. Yet this is never the case. People and relationships do not remain status quo. If you stay frozen and do not take steps to change your situation, you are **making a decision** to let your life be dictated by outside forces. You are relinquishing what power you do have in your relationship and making a choice to sentence yourself to life in a marital quagmire. The tension you feel is a warning light. Use it as a signal to initiate constructive change in your relationship.

If you do choose to make changes, recognize that those alterations can also lead to pain. Ideally, you would get the support for your efforts from your spouse, children, parents, and friends. However, sometimes that doesn't happen, and instead they may attempt to restore you to your *old self.* No matter how uncomfortable things may have been, the old equilibrium often feels safer for others than risking unpredictable change. They may even encourage the altered behavior verbally, but then subtly sabotage your efforts by imposing numerous roadblocks. No matter how positive the change might be for your own well-being, do not expect applause, or even appreciation, from others. You must make these changes for yourself, not for anyone else.

If you seek advice or feedback from friends or family, be aware that they are not *unbiased* observers. They are viewing your situation through their own not-so-neutral kaleidoscope. This is especially true of friends who are recently divorced or separated, or those who are unhappy in their own relationships. It is your life, and ultimately the decisions are yours to make. You know your feelings and you know your own situation better then anyone alive. Do not let your choices be dictated by others. If you have doubts, seek professional counseling. Whether the outside advice comes from professional sources, friends, or family, accept their feedback and counsel, and then **you** choose your own path.

Whatever decisions you make in your marriage, keep in mind that they are the best decisions you are capable of at the moment you make them. In retrospect, given more information, more time to evaluate, and a different emotional state, it is always easy to second-guess yourself. If you do regret a decision, do not chastize yourself for your lack of perfection. Instead, use it as a learning experience. Again, at the time of your decision, you made the best choice you could.

## Seeking Counseling

Our goal has been to teach you some of the key skills and essential concepts vital to building a marriage. However, we have purposely not tackled some of the complex issues that relationships become embroiled in, such as sexual dysfunctions, addictions, extramarital relationships, problems with children, parents, or in-laws. Each of these would separately require a volume to cover adequately. By using the tools we have provided you with, and by doing some of the supplementary reading recommended at the end of this book, you will be able to resolve most marital problems. However, if the use of these tools does not lead to a resolution of the issues after a short period of time, we recommend that you seek counseling.

Counseling may seem like an expensive alternative, but your personal suffering is a much higher price to pay. Both of the authors of this book are well acquainted with the plight of couples who have suffered needlessly for years with a dysfunctional marriage only to find their issues were solvable within a matter of weeks after they sought professional counseling. If you choose to seek counseling, get a recommendation for a qualified counselor from a friend who has undergone successful counseling or from a professional whom you respect. Another alternative is to check the yellow pages under the headings of *Psychologists* or *Marriage Counselors*. Do not hesitate to call more than one counselor. Shop, ask questions, and compare as you might with any major life decision, but do not allow price to be the prime determinant.

Even if your marital situation is serious enough that you are not certain whether or not you wish to remain in the relationship, counseling is still appropriate. Your ac-

tive participation in counseling is not a commitment to
stay in the relationship. All you are promising when you
enter into counseling is that you are willing to make an
effort to explore your inner self and your marital relationship. Make a choice to give a 100 percent effort to
resolve your marital difficulties. That way you will know
that whatever decision you make, it is the best one possible. If you choose to leave your relationship without
giving it a fair chance, you will always have some doubt
as to whether a harmonious outcome could have been
possible.

---

### EXERCISE 29

Look through the notes you have kept for the past
twenty-eight days and summarize what changes you
have made in your behavior and note in what ways
you feel different. Then note any changes your partner has made.

Pay special attention to the fact that any *mistakes*
you have made during the course of the exercises
have not been wasted. Rather, they have ultimately
been used as learning tools.

# Storybook Marriages

Life is not a fairy tale. Your world will inevitably include a regular dose of serious bumps and major crises. What this book offers you are the tools to transform those bumps and those crises into opportunities to further deepen and enrich your relationship.

Fantasy relationships that we see on television or in the movies are truly fiction. They are visual fairy tales. Even though we sometimes understand and empathize with the characters, they are strictly fictional. It is interesting to watch episodes of such old-time TV programs as "I Love Lucy." Millions of viewers adored Lucy and Ricky's storybook relationship, and no doubt many modeled their relationship after this famous couple. During every episode the two of them would get into all sorts of outrageous difficulties, and they always managed to resolve their problems and restore their harmonious relationship. Yet, if you really examine their relationship, Lucy and Ricky were constantly engaged in a power struggle, handled through mutual trickery and deceit. They engaged in very little teamwork, there was little honest sharing, and there was virtually no effective listening. In the real world, this relationship would have been a disaster waiting to happen.

We offer no magic solutions, or instant turnarounds. The marriage we have presented to you is a model based on teamwork, open communication, and flexibility—a partnership where resolving differences takes precedence over winning or losing. A marriage where *errors* are encouraged as a part of the learning process. It is a relationship where effective listening and sharing are the highest priorities while judging and controlling are among the lowest. And it is a relationship in which most of the skills that form the basic building blocks are learnable.

You are the director of your own marital destiny. What you elect to build with the building blocks you have been given is up to you. Whether or not you choose to change your relationship at this time, you have been given one unalterable and undeniable gift: a new lens for your kaleidoscope—a new perspective that has inalterably affected your view of your marriage and your marital partner.

---

### EXERCISE 30

Write down three changes you would like to begin to make in the next thirty days. Specifically outline the steps you intend to take in order to implement these changes. These do not have to be changes in the relationship. They can simply be changes you would like to make in yourself. Ultimately, if you are happier, your relationship will benefit.

# Appendix A

## *Feelings Chart*

"I feel" followed by an adjective or an adverb identifies a feeling. Example: I feel sad.

If you can substitute "I think" for "I feel," it is not a feeling. It is a judgment. Example: I feel that you are angry with me.

| | | | |
|---|---|---|---|
| SAD | Guilty | Bashful | Bored |
| | Ashamed | Stupid | Sleepy |
| | Depressed | Miserable | Inferior |
| | Lonely | Inadequate | Apathetic |
| PEACEFUL | Content | Pensive | Trusting |
| | Thoughtful | Relaxed | Nurturing |
| | Intimate | Responsive | Sentimental |
| | Loving | Serene | Thankful |
| POWERFUL | Faithful | Cheerful | Respected |
| | Important | Satisfied | Proud |
| | Hopeful | Valuable | Intelligent |
| | Appreciated | Worthwhile | Confident |

| JOYFUL | Excited | Daring | Creative |
| | Sexy | Fascinating | Aware |
| | Energetic | Stimulating | Extravagant |
| | Playful | Amused | Delighted |
| | | | |
| SCARED | Rejected | Bewildered | Insecure |
| | Confused | Discouraged | Anxious |
| | Helpless | Insignificant | Foolish |
| | Submissive | Weak | Embarrassed |
| | | | |
| MAD | Hurt | Jealous | Hateful |
| | Hostile | Selfish | Critical |
| | Angry | Frustrated | Irritated |
| | Rage | Furious | Skeptical |

# Appendix C

## ALTERNATIVE EXERCISE
## FOR DAY 18

Take a half-hour for yourself. Undress and stand in front of a mirror, preferably one that is full-length. Look at yourself from head to toe, without any judgments. Using a lotion or a powder, caress yourself as you would your partner. Touch every inch of your body, feeling the texture, the contours, and the temperature. Touch as you would a fur rug or a soft pet. Take a special look at those areas you consider flawed: stretch marks, scars, etc. Touch them with tenderness. Look at each feature and say to yourself, *"I accept you and love you."* It may sound awkward and silly, but the self-acceptance is very important.

# Appendix D

## ALTERNATIVE EXERCISE
## FOR DAY 20

Write down three things you resent about your partner and three things you appreciate about your partner. When you have completed that, complete the following sentence: *I choose not to share my resentments and my appreciations with my partner because* . . .

Finally, choose a friend you trust and share all the resentments and appreciations, as well as the reason you chose not to share them with your partner.

# Appendix E

## ALTERNATIVE EXERCISE
## FOR DAY 22

Do this exercise with a friend you trust.

Pick a topic that you and your partner have recently disagreed about or have argued about in the past. It may even be one that is still being disagreed upon. Stage a mock argument, with you playing the role of your partner and your friend playing you. Try to choose similar arguments to those your mate might pick, and act out his or her mannerisms during an argument. Feel free to exaggerate. It often makes this type of role-playing more fun. You will have to brief your friend beforehand on how you would be likely to act during an argument.

After you have played out the argument, share with each other how it felt to be in the other's shoes.

# Appendix F

## COMMUNICATION RULES

*Rule 1: If your partner appears absorbed in something else, at a time when you want to talk, request that he/she listen to you or have your spouse suggest an alternative time.*

*Rule 2: When sharing concerns or feelings with your partner, begin your statements with "I," or preferably "I feel (sad, angry, etc.)."*

*Rule 3: Be clear in stating what you want, rather than expressing what you don't want.*

*Rule 4: Rather than asking questions, rephrase them as statements that reflect your feelings.*

*Rule 5: When engaging in any discussion, avoid the use of statements which tend to drag up the past. One effective way of limiting these kinds of statements is avoid the use of absolutes: words such as "always," "never," "whenever," "every time."*

*Rule 6: Be consistent in both your words and your actions. If you or your partner notice inconsistencies,*

Continued

*assess whether the multiple messages represent conflicting feelings within you.*

*Rule 7: Let your partner know that you are listening attentively. If you are not ready to fully attend to what your partner is saying, give him/her an alternative time when you will be totally available.*

*Rule 8: Clarify what you have heard.*

*Rule 9: Listen without interrupting.*

*Rule 10: Keep an open mind when listening to your partner's point of view, then reassess your own position, using all the information at your disposal.*

*Rule 11: No matter how much you disagree with your partner, do not judge or ridicule his/her opinion. Accept his/her right to hold a differing belief. If you wish to share your differing opinion, first, clarify what you understand your partner to be saying. Let your mate know that you accept it as his/her opinion. Then, share your own belief.*

# Recommended Reading

## *Addiction*

Carnes, Patrick. *Out of the Shadows.* Minneapolis: CompCare, 1983.

Sexual addiction is finally "out of the closet." A pioneering account with illuminating case histories.

Johnson, Vernon. *I'll Quit Tomorrow.* San Francisco: Harper & Row, Revised 1980.

An in-depth guide to identifying and treating alcoholism. May be a little "heavy" but includes a comprehensive view of the progression of alcoholism and the process of recovery.

Katherine, Anne. *Anatomy of a Food Addiction: The Brain Chemistry of Overeating.* New York: Prentice-Hall, 1991.

A thorough and up-to-date look at this still misunderstood addiction.

Roche, Helena. *The Addiction Process: From Enabling to Intervention.* Deerfield Beach, Florida: Health Communications, 1990.

Comprehensively covers all the addictions. Helps identify the underlying problems.

Roth, Geneen. *Breaking Free from Compulsive Overeating.* New York: Signet, 1984.

   Suggests practical ways to stop compulsive overeating. Roth also examines the folly of dieting and the importance of nurturing.

### Co-dependency

Bach, George, and Deutsch, Ronald M. *Stop, You're Driving Me Crazy.* New York: Berkley Books, 1981.

   We classify this under co-dependency because, though Bach is a master at communication, this book is also a rich experiential account of how to avoid getting absorbed by the needs of others.

Beattie, Melody. *Co-dependent No More.* New York: Hazeldon, 1987.

   A book resplendent with stories to which co-dependents can relate, especially if their spouses are alcoholic.

————*Beyond Co-dependency.* San Francisco: Harper & Row, 1989.

   A good look at problems co-dependents face and nurturing ways to avoid those difficulties.

————*The Language of Letting Go: Daily Meditations for Co-dependents.* New York: Hazeldon, 1990.

   One of a series of meditation books in the Hazeldon series. Encourages daily reflection on typical co-dependent dilemmas and contains insights as to how co-dependents can take care of themselves.

Melody, Pia, with Miller, Andrea Wells, and Miller, Judith. *Facing Co-dependency.* San Francisco: Harper & Row, 1989.

   A thorough look at the roots and origins of co-dependency. Especially helpful for therapists.

Forward, Susan, and Buck, Craig. *When Passion Holds You Prisoner.* New York: Bantam, 1991.

   Practical, straightforward suggestions on how people get themselves into destructive relationships and how they can get out of them.

### Divorce

Colgrove, Melba; Bloomfield, Harold; and McWilliam, Peter. *How to Survive the Loss of a Love.* New York: Bantam, 1991.
Daily affirmations, survival poems, and sayings for anyone who has lost someone special.

Trafford, Abigail. *Crazy Time.* New York: Bantam, 1982.
Dynamite little book. A very personal account about what to expect in that roller coaster aftermath following a divorce.

### Family of Origin Issues

Bradshaw, John. *The Family.* Deerfield Beach, Florida: Health Communications, 1988.
Bradshaw's award-winning book takes a close look at how family of origin issues and different family styles impact us as adults.

———*Healing the Shame that Binds You.* New York: Bantam, 1988.
A penetrating examination of shame as the root of all addictions.

———*Homecoming: Reclaiming and Championing Your Inner Child.* New York: Bantam, 1990.
Excellent step-by-step workbook that takes you back through your childhood and helps you reclaim the missing stages, which you may have blocked or repressed.

Black, Claudia. *It Will Never Happen to Me.* Denver: MAC Publishing, 1981.
This is one of the first ACOA (Adult Children of Alcoholics) books. It is told from a personal point of view by a therapist who comes from, and works extensively with, this population. Clear and easy to read.

Miller, Alice. *Drama of the Gifted Child: Prisoners of Childhood.* New York: Basic Books, 1981.
Tough reading but worth it if you want an in-depth understanding of how creative, sensitive children get squelched by rigid child-raising methods.

————*Banished Knowledge: Facing Childhood Injuries.* New York: Doubleday, 1990.

Controversial, stimulating, and provocative. Alice Miller once again challenges us not to take for granted the sufferings of our own childhood, so we will not repeat the same injustices when raising our own children.

Miller, Joy, and Ripper, Marianne. *Following the Yellow Brick Road: The Adult Child's Personal Journey Through Oz.* Deerfield Beach, Florida: Health Communications, 1988.

Using characters from *The Wizard of Oz*, the authors cleverly compare different family roles that people get thrust upon them—usually early in childhood. They give some helpful guidelines for how to get out of those roles.

### Intimacy

Bach, George, and Wyden, Peter. *The Intimate Enemy.* New York: Avon, 1968.

Provocative and rich with case studies. Bach explodes the myth that fighting destroys a marriage. Instead he suggests that "fair fighting" increases intimacy and is an integral part of a solid relationship. A must for marriage counselors.

Goldhor-Lerner, Harriet, Ph.D. *The Dance of Intimacy.* New York: Harper & Row, 1989.

Well written. Great examples of how we thirst for, pursue, and then withdraw in our pursuit of intimacy.

### Men

Bly, Robert. *Iron John.* Reading, PA: Addison Wesley, 1990.

Bly has a rambling, witty, story-telling style that will resound deeply with men who've lost a father to work, death, or alcohol.

Keen, Sam. *Fire in the Belly.* New York: Bantam, 1991.

Engaging, personal and vibrant. Keen's description of a man's journey is helpful and inspiring.

## Money

Felton-Collins, Victoria. *Couples and Money: Why Money Interferes and What To Do About It.* New York: Bantam, 1990.

Collins has done a fine job in exploring the issues behind money problems. Better yet, she offers practical solutions.

## Parenting

Gale, Jay, Ph.D. *A Parent's Guide to Teenage Sexuality.* New York: Henry Holt, 1989.

Practical, easy-to-read guide for parents who need a no-nonsense approach to everyday situations and problems that accompany teenage sexuality.

Ginott, H. G. *Between Parent and Child.* New York: Avon, 1956; and *Between Parent and Teenager.* New York: Avon, 1969.

Ginott is still the best there is at teaching basic communication with and realistic expectations of kids. His teenager book gives fine examples of typical situations with which parents are confronted.

Gordon, Thomas. *P.E.T.* New York: Wyden, 1970.

An easy-to-understand method of parent training taught to thousands of mothers and fathers across the country.

Mason, Daniel A. *Double Duty: Parenting Our Kids While Reparenting Ourselves.* Minneapolis: CompCare, 1990.

As the title suggests, the author is offering some refreshing insights and tools for those who have to relearn how to take care of themselves while raising their own children.

O'Gorman, Patricia, and Diaz, Philip Oliver. *Breaking the Cycle of Addiction: A Parent's Guide to Raising Healthy Kids.* Deerfield Beach, Florida: Health Communications, 1987.

This book is ideal for recovering parents who want to stop the pattern from continuing with their own children.

### Parents of Adults

Ashner, Laurie, and Meyerson, Mitch. *When Parents Love To[o]
Much.* New York: Avon, 1990.
> Teaches you how to extricate yourself from the guilt an[d]
> demands of parents who can't let go of you, without d[e]
> stroying either you or them.

Bloomfield, Harold. *Making Peace with Your Parents.* Ne[w]
York: Ballantine, 1983.
> One of the early self-help books on healing your relatio[n]
> ship with your parents. Still timely and lively, with gre[at]
> examples.

Forward, Susan, with Buck, Craig. *Toxic Parents: Overcomi[ng]
Their Hurtful Legacy and Reclaiming Your Life.* New York: Ba[n]
tam, 1989.
> An excellent, practical guide for dealing with the legacy [of]
> pain left by overtly and subtly abusive parents. Step-by-ste[p]
> examples for every situation.

### Psychotherapy

Kopp, Sheldon. *If You Meet the Buddha on the Road, Kill Hi[m.]
New York: Bantam, 1972.
> A masterpiece on how our growth as a people parallels o[ur]
> spiritual growth. Kopp shows us how therapy will make [us]
> free only if we are willing to be brutally honest with ou[r]
> selves and others.

———*The End of Innocence.* New York: Vantage, 1990.
> In this slim volume, Kopp cuts to the core of the myth ma[ny]
> of us want to cling to: "If I'm good, life will be fair."

Peck, M. Scott. *The Road Less Traveled.* New York: Simon [&]
Schuster, 1978.
> An enlightening journey. Told from the therapist's point [of]
> view, it recounts how the therapeutic process works best.

Viorst, Judith. *Necessary Losses.* New York: Fawcett, 1986.
> A thorough examination of the life passages we must a[ll]
> experience. Viorst helps us see that we can grow rather tha[n]
> be victimized by change. She captures the feelings of ang[er]

and ecstasy from the time we leave the security of the womb to the time we face our own mortality.

## Sexual Abuse

Davis, Laura. *Courage to Heal Workbook for Women and Men Survivors of Sexual Abuse.* New York: Harper & Row, 1990.
A very extensive workbook for survivors of sexual abuse. It is best used with a therapist or survivors' support group.

## Sexuality

Barbach, Lonnie. *For Yourself: The Fulfillment of Female Sexuality.* New York: Doubleday, 1975.
Still one of the best books for women looking for a practical and experiential way to explore their own sexuality.
————*For Each Other: Sharing Sexual Intimacy.* New York: Doubleday, 1982.
Barbach takes some of the technical information on sexuality and makes it readily accessible for couples. Good experiential exercises.

Hite, Shere. *The Hite Report.* New York: Dell, 1981.
Originally a master's thesis, which turned into a best-seller, it gives anecdotal results of a survey of the sexual practices and beliefs of a cross section of women across the nation.

Yaffe, Maurice, and Fenwick, Elizabeth. *Sexual Happiness: A Practical Approach.* New York: Henry Holt, 1988.
An excellent reference for anyone trying to reach an understanding about their own sexual difficulties.

Zilbergeld, Bernie. *Male Sexuality.* Boston: Little, Brown, 1978.
Still the best for anyone who wants to understand the sexual pressures and expectations with which men struggle. Contains good information about male sexual dysfunctions. Frank, humorous, and very informative.

Gallwey, W. Timothy. *The Inner Game of Tennis.* New York: Random House, 1974.
Although written for tennis players, this book explains what happens when you try too hard at any physical endeavor.

For men who suffer from impotency or women who have trouble reaching an orgasm, it may be the easiest-to-understand book about performance pressures.

### Women

Dowling, Colette. *Cinderella Complex.* New York: Pocket Books, 1981.

Good research about how women have bought into the myth that they will be taken care of. The cure: self-love and a willingness to take care of themselves.

Freedman, Rita. *Body Love: A Practical Guide for Women.* New York: Harper & Row, 1989.

Explores how outer looks can be really appreciated by seeing your inner self. Essential reading for women who are critical of their own bodies.

Goldhor-Lerner, Harriet, Ph.D. *The Dance of Anger.* New York: Harper & Row, 1985.

A wonderful exploration showing what happens to women who don't express anger appropriately and how this impacts on their ability to have an intimate relationship.

Norwood, Robin. *Women Who Love Too Much.* New York: Pocket Books, 1985.

This was one of the first self-help books for women who give themselves away in a relationship. Great recovery stories and an examination of the lives of women who have lived this drama.

Sanford, Linda, and Donovan, Mary Ellen. *Women and Self-Esteem.* New York: Penguin, 1986.

This a rich, anecdotal book analyzing why many women think of themselves in such a negative way. Better yet, this book offers chapter-by-chapter exercises for change.

Shainess, Natalie. *Sweet Suffering.* New York: Pocket Books, 1984.

A gem of a book for women who want out of the seductive trap of martyrdom.